Freedom

from
the **I**

Ultimate Path to a
Free Mind and Real Success

Shashank Kasliwal

JAICO PUBLISHING HOUSE

Ahmedabad Bangalore Bhopal Bhubaneswar Chennai
Delhi Hyderabad Kolkata Lucknow Mumbai

Published by Jaico Publishing House
A-2 Jash Chambers, 7-A Sir Phirozshah Mehta Road
Fort, Mumbai - 400 001
jaicopub@jaicobooks.com
www.jaicobooks.com

FREEDOM FROM THE I
ISBN 978-93-86867-48-3

First Jaico Impression: 2018
Third Jaico Impression: 2019

Page design and layout: Special Effects, Mumbai

To my father & mother – living examples of unlimited inner power,
and to my family and friends for being patient when I wasn't.

This book will help people live without psychological trauma. Love each other or perish.

— **Salim Khan**
Actor & Script Writer

Since his childhood, Shashank has been very confident, self-made and capable of overcoming the challenges of life. Through this book, he has shared his ideologies and strategies how to come out of psychological sufferings, which many of us have to go through. I am sure his book will be a guiding star to the readers passing through similar phases in life.

— **Dr. Naresh Aggarwal**
International President, Lions Club International, USA

Freedom from the I is a profound and thoughtful book based on Kasliwalji's personal experiences and search for the true nature of life and being. I'm sure it will help many people to make their lives more creative, productive and harmonious.

— **Kabir Bedi**
Actor

A guidebook to someone who wishes to change his/her life and seek tranquillity. A must read for all.

— **Anil Rai Gupta**
Chairman & Managing Director, Havells India Ltd.

Out of suffering comes consciousness and energy beyond thought. Debut author Shashank Kasliwal reveals that thought is the victim of conditioning and to break free we need to stop looking back and observe. Sensitive. Substantial. Sparkling.

— **Bhawana Somaaya**
Journalist & Film Expert

Shashank is a dynamic and enthusiastic motivator. I can't praise him enough for the brilliant job of writing this book on one of the toughest topics, i.e., self-awareness.

— **Dr. S.B. Singh**
Senior Advisor, Policy Advisory Services, Ernst & Young LLP

Congratulations to Shashank for such an initiative. It's a very important topic and I am sure this book will help professionals to break free from the shackles of the ego and self-centered attitude.

— Ajay Sevekari
Executive Director, Bridgestone India

This book will be a guiding light for millennial generation as they enter corporate life as it guides us to work in teams without stress and with mutual trust and respect.

— Sudarshan Surana
Managing Director, Accenture, North Carolina, USA

This [book] will bring clarity to the way people think. I recommend this book to one and all.

— Sonal Desai
Former Executive Director, Hindustan Petroleum Corporation Limited

A book gripping enough to take you back into "finding of oneself" ... engrossing and gripping way of [story] telling..."

— Amit Sharma
Head of Procurement, Daimler India Commercial Vehicles Pvt. Ltd.

This is [about] basic training for the mind, the heart and the soul. Reading Freedom from the I is the most positive transforming experience I've ever been a part of.

— Rahul Gupta
Regional Head, Maharashtra, ICICI Bank

This book prompts us to look at life experiences in a detached way. It provides the necessary insight that can liberate us from painful memories and peep into a bright energetic future.

— Archana Yemeshvary
Chief Manager, Organization Development
Hindustan Petroleum Corporation Limited

Nicely captured and interestingly assembled block by block, a new perspective on life. This Book is very relevant to new-age professionals.

— **Umesh Shrivastava**
Head Operations, Ultratech Cements, Aditya Birla Group

The book is just magnificent. It dwells characteristically into the much-needed emotional insight about the fellow beings; the time spent [with this book] and the questions that were answered were simply beautiful.

— **Lav Sharma**
*Plant Human Resources Head (Haridwar & Vadodara),
Hero MotoCorp Ltd.*

An eye-opener and a book that truly speaks to your soul.

— **Supriya Pandit**
Deputy Manager, Human Resources, Mafatlal Group

Shashank is a facilitator striving from within to make other people's dreams come true."

— **Sanjay Trivedi**
Deputy General Manager, Human Resources, MAN Trucks India Pvt. Ltd.

It's rare to come across a book so well written and connecting. It seems like my own story.

— **Shikha Verma**
HRD, Honda Cars India Limited

Fly high with this book as it keeps you light when you practice the techniques mentioned to use the mind and not get used by it.

— **Rajat Rana**
International Pilot, Air India

ability to direct the flow of energy in a positive direction.

You will develop a new way of looking at things, that is, with a *whole perception* and not *fragmented perception* based on only past experience. You would not have to replace a negative pattern with a positive one but it will drop on its own without any effort with the presence of consciousness and in the absence of the ego.

How to use this book

This book will be like a ready reckoner, telling you where you need to take action and where you should refrain from blindly following egoistic dictates in order to activate the forces within. There are times when we just get through people, things, meetings and nothing seems to stop us. We are dynamic in the face of situations and feel like we can handle anything that life throws at us. This particular energy can be created just by knowing the right buttons to push or not.

If things seem repetitive, please keep in mind that they are purposefully written in that manner to get the point straight inside your heart, bypassing your mind. Second, if you are too logical and read out of context then many a times you will feel that there are contradicting statements. Delve into the *why* of things rather than only seeing it from your perspective, which is always limited.

Third, avoid reading with judgmental eyes or from the domain of *right* and *wrong*, work together with me on this journey. Enjoy the process and it will help you get where you want to be and also help you discover it if you don't know where you want to be. Only a life of purpose is a meaningful life.

In short, the process in this book will free you from the constraints of the past and rid you of that ego, which doesn't let you see things clearly. This will help you expose your blind spots,

However, the problem is not the fear, insecurity or hunger for power and dominance, but the very mechanism resulting in these strong emotions.

The only way to end this everlasting suffering is to recognise and free ourselves from that which is keeping us imprisoned, the EGO. With this book, you will be able to see the different ways in which the ego makes us think, speak and act, and it will help you eliminate the conditioned processes of the mind that perpetuate suffering.

You don't even realise how the ego takes over pretending to be you. You are not who you think you are. Who you think you are, is a notion created by your ego. The suffering ends when you become conscious about this unconscious process and realise that people don't function by themselves but are instead being controlled by the ego. The easiest way to see through your ego is to become aware of its impact on your body, on your relationships and the way you perceive situations and deal with challenges. The darkness spread by the ego can be removed by the light of consciousness. The moment you get in touch with this *consciousness*, you feel the freedom to change the negative patterns that keep you in their clutches; freedom to respond with calmness and kindness even when others are angry or hostile; and simply, freedom to enjoy whatever life brings.

In the process of going through this book, you will come face to face with a lot of faults within you. During such times, don't despair but rejoice. These faults have been in you all along but once you accept them, their ill-effects will subside without you having to change anything. The very ability to see them will free you from the mental patterns created by your own ego. Freeing yourself from these faults means freeing yourself from negative karmic patterns that are formed due to the energy generated by past thoughts and actions. This understanding gives us control over the subconscious patterns that control our perception, behaviour, action and the how we are trying to run away from our present. This leads to a permanent state of suffering in many people. We all go through failures, heartbreaks, sickness, old age and death of near and dear ones. The biggest lesson is learning to handle ourselves during these eventualities.

Due to psychological suffering, you feel small despite having a full-grown body. You then try to feel superior by earning money and respect. Can we clear our minds first? Your wishes tell you what is missing. Listen to them. You have these wishes because you are trying to fill some vacuum or emptiness inside. This also affects your behaviour. Our behaviour is the most trusted indicator of self-awareness. It's important to identify what makes you feel bad, why you isolate yourself and what triggers you.

We live in times where there is increasing pressure to perform and a rush to experience happiness but at the same time, we do not have the will or the energy to do so. We are all stuck in our own problems. Our performance, creativity and engagement are suffering as a result.

A Strategy to Approach a Problem Before it Approaches Us

Now the question is, shall we approach a problem with our prejudiced notions, point of views, opinions and pre-existing mindsets or can there be some other way as well. We have tried our ways to resolve these concerns and difficulties before but have rarely succeeded, and the purpose of living continues to elude us. We think our problems are because of spouses, parents, friends, bosses, our jobs, but it is actually deeper than it looks. We refuse to face the reality and live in a make-believe world, ignorant of the cause of our suffering.

Preface

Psychologically we all suffer, and to end this suffering we must know the essential issue of our life – the imbalance between inner and outer freedom. Our material possessions are growing, but we are still not contented, as a matter of fact, our suffering is increasing by the day. Irrespective of our money, power, positions and personalities, each one of us suffers psychologically. The problem begins when there is no freedom – freedom from inner conflicts, aggression, confusion, jealousy, lack of deep insight and intuitiveness, which then gets expressed externally in our behaviour with people and the way we work and act in situations. Today, a majority of the people are restless and feel like a victim of something or someone. Unless and until we dig a little deeper into the root cause of things, it will be difficult to live a successful life as motivation doesn't last long. But once you get to the cause of your demotivation, you are free and inspired for life.

The aim of this book is neither analysis nor synthesis but transcendence. It is to go beyond the troubling mind. It is not work within the mind; it is work that takes you outside the disturbing mind. The idea is to develop the ability to stay unaffected despite your mental conditioning, to free you from negative energy and get you to a state where nothing impacts you, a life that is not only focused on earning money and respect but going beyond. Not brushing things away unseen, but taking them out and handling them powerfully. Many of us have no energy as all our energy is blocked by our desires and spent in complaining most of the times. Why do people across the world run after pleasure? Actively seeking pleasure, like waiting for a break or a holiday, demonstrates solutions and struggling with every situation, I found a reservoir of energy inside myself, the energy that had the power to free the mind. I relaxed as the noise inside ceased, the challenges of life started disappearing and I started becoming blissful. This calm state allowed me to focus and I started doing well at work with less effort and more ease. It struck me like lightning – peace generates creativity and in turn allows one to prosper as creativity helps in handling challenges, situations, people and even one's own limiting beliefs.

Everybody goes through difficult situations but few learn and learn enough to make an action plan from it to create something for the next level. You have to go through hell to know the way to heaven. I would not be writing this had I not gone through heartbreaks. Your journey through hell shows you that heaven is buried deep within, only shielded by your desire for it. I went through hell; you need not, provided you awaken your intelligence. Life can be blissful; we just need to learn to activate our dormant energy. This book will help you radically transform your life. Get back your energy, stamina and the power to enjoy the bliss that life is.

undisturbed peace and energy that will lead to a great life. You can stop feeling suppressed, repressed and depressed the moment you accept that the creator is inside you. Earlier, I used to suppress the negative feelings by distracting myself through work and parties but now I have become *patiently restless* to handle it. That is, instead of avoiding experiencing these feelings, I embraced them and eagerly handled them by just letting myself be. I was still wary of my emotions but this time, I found myself in them. By losing my family, friends, society and work, I found that everything I needed was and has always been inside me.

I started getting little insights into what was to be changed. I stopped looking outside for approval and praise. I took a good look at myself and every part of myself that I didn't like. I started opening up every wound I was carrying, but had brushed under the carpet. I took responsibility for my life, for everything and everybody connected to me. With time I started feeling responsible for those who were not even connected to me. I started connecting with animals, plants and everything else around me. I faced all the anger, jealousy, sadness, anxieties, fears and insecurities that crossed my way without evaluating and criticizing, and just observing and letting them be. I went with the flow by not resisting myself, I cried when I felt like it and laughed till my belly ached when it came from the heart. Somewhere inside this made me peaceful and I understood what real authenticity is. I understood meditation by being meditative all the time, which made me truly peaceful, as opposed to just sitting with my eyes closed. This was new to me as I was not meditating to tell people about it. Clue after clue came to me as I learned about myself. The pendulum that the mind is, its oscillations between my past and my future slowed, leaving me to enjoy the present I, was getting more aware of my inner self.

For the first time, I experienced mindfulness. Not 'full' literally, in fact, it was now empty of the torment. Instead of using cosmetic

When my sufferings came to the fore, I stopped meeting everybody, went for vipassana meditation and took only as much work as I got on its own. In this phase, I realised that in spite of being alone, I still had the same problems. I was still complaining about my girlfriend, friends, parents and work in my private theatre, my mind. It was a eureka moment for me and for the first time I felt I was alive. It came like an insight that the problem was not money or honey, but it was "I", "me" and "myself". I could clearly see that there were no people or trying circumstances in my days of vipassana but the feeling of helplessness was still there. I experienced in those moments of distress that there were two identities inside me, one constantly telling me what to do, what not to do and the other choosing from the options and eventually suffering because of this inner conflict.

I call this a eureka moment because it made me find my own buttons, my own remote control to make me free, happy and successful, which had nothing to do with external situations, events and people. As a matter of fact, the very expectation from people and situations was making me sad and making me lose focus on what I wanted to do. Nothing external had changed with this realisation, everything was the same, but the way I looked at everything transformed.

Intuitively I knew what I wanted. I simply wanted a peaceful life as I was so disturbed psychologically that lack of money looked like a minuscule problem relatively. I just wanted to enjoy myself, enjoy life and not just keep gathering useless material possessions as and when my mind's incessant chatter so dictated. I understood that going through so much anxiety, insecurity, unnecessary stress and tension is futile. I finally saw the reason for the mess I was in, because of which I was reacting to people and situations in such a hostile manner. I experienced that if one properly handles day-to-day situations, what people say and do and our own negative thoughts which always come in the way, one can experience

My health began to deteriorate and my energy dipped, too. I had put on lot a of weight and felt as if I had suddenly started aging. There was no area of my life that I was satisfied with.

One day, out of curiosity and perhaps to find someone like me I asked many people if they, too, went through what I was going through. I felt angry, upset, depressed and sad almost every time things didn't go my way. And my expectations were so high that getting my way was nearly impossible. I asked myself: *Am I forever going to depend on situations and other people to feel good?* I felt as if I was shrinking and many times I avoided meeting people. I retreated into my shell. To my astonishment, a majority of the people, after much cajoling, admitted to me that they feel almost the same way. And in an attempt to get out of all this – the sorrow, the sadness – they earn money to raise their self-respect so they feel good about themselves. They take foreign trips; consume alcohol and other toxic substances. The majority also said that they felt good when they were appreciated by other people and when they earned a lot of money. The problem was that they only momentarily felt good because of those material things. When I was enquiring, they too realized that these pleasures were not going to last for long and it's an ongoing struggle to be happy. **I was awakened to the fact that instead of working on the state we were in, we were all trying to run away from it and covering it up through various means.** During those times, I read a lot of spiritual texts, attended innumerable training sessions and understood things conceptually. I had answers to everybody's problems, except mine. I started remaining angry almost during all situations, especially while dealing with people.

The more pathetic and sad I felt, the tougher life and situations became.

and each and every challenge raised inside of me something that was almost palpable. I realised that becoming aware of the impact of what is happening is waking up. It took me a good while to understand that whatever was happening to me was a result of my own thoughts. They were either past worries or imaginary fears about the future creating havoc in my present life. The tremendous pressure of suffering compelled my consciousness to pull back from its identification with the sad and fearful ego, which was nothing but just a fiction of the mind.

Waking up to your true self requires letting go of the false one, of who you imagined yourself to be.

This is my story but you will find some part of me in you. I have regained my true self from the dominating thoughts of the material world and have moved on to discerning pure wisdom. This wisdom has the potential to create the mental, physical, emotional and spiritual worlds that each one of us craves for.

On my journey I realised that these weren't deliberate, conscious thoughts that made me miserable, they were merely an outcome of my conditioning. I wasn't creating these thoughts; they were getting created on their own because of the way my mind functioned.

I was awakened to the fact that instead of working on the state we were in, we were all trying to run away from it and covering it up through various means.

After all, who wants to live in misery? Majority of the times I felt unwanted, like someone not inviting me to an event, passing a rude comment, not responding to my phone calls, not replying to my messages, not getting enough work, work orders getting cancelled and on top of that, fights with my girlfriend, parents and siblings had become routine, too. Eventually, I had no place to live after having fought with my father and was barely earning any money at the age of 36.

Summary

This book is about my journey. I was born into a rich family but before I could experience these inherited riches, we had become poor. Poor only in terms of money, because for me, something had started to change from within, something that helped me handle people, situations and life's challenges with confidence. My surroundings seemed to be telling me that you are the money that you have but something inside was telling me that I am more than what people saw me as. There is more to life than what those cold eyes reflected. But this was only the beginning of the process, and it wasn't easy.

I was fed up with feeling small, the way I used to feel about insignificant things, the mood swings, irritation, anger, frustration, heartbreak and that unavoidable sinking feeling. All this somewhere disturbed my energy and I lost focus, performing poorly no matter what I did and finally felt as if I was failing and falling in life. Till then I had lived my whole life under the burden of anxiety and insecurity, always trying to be somewhere else. I would get annoyed with people over petty issues, get agitated and sulk. I would not confront them straight up and tell them what I felt bad about but rather my entire behaviour towards them would change. After a lot of introspection, I clearly saw that I was living in denial mode. I felt rejected by people because of which I shut out others, feeling miserable by myself.

I suffered to no extent. Though to understand suffering, it was important to go through it. I realised that if we don't get our lives in order, our acts will have no meaning. I not only wanted my misery to end but help others end theirs too. I became highly sensitive self-created limits and values that act as barriers and do not let you experience the vibrant world around you.

You will start seeing events of your life like a blueprint connecting each dot towards your ultimate goal. Life gives you indirect and direct messages through various events. One just has to be conscious about his own energy to receive the directions, see if it is in sync with life or not. Your energy increases when you work in harmony with your nature. You don't have to go to an astrologer to know the right time; the resulting peace in your internal life will convert all the wrongs into rights. Knowing there is a destiny is good, believing in destiny is bad. 'Cosmic will' can be seen with the rising sun, the rotating earth, in your very breath but at the same time you can also experience 'free will' and choose to experience this stunning life once you get out of the wrong way of living.

Are you ready to go to the next level?

Contents

1

The False in You

There are many people who are quite accomplished – they possess the objects of their desires, are in the relationships they had always wanted to be in, have jobs and have the riches and health they had hoped for. Yet, they suffer from deep-rooted fears, anxieties, sorrow and pain. You rarely see happy, vibrant faces that are full of life without alcohol.

Why are people unhappy and aimlessly chasing pleasure despite all their achievements and possessions?

Is it that we always want and desire something instead of enjoying what we already have? If you see, the desires we have by default bring along suffering and pain because they arise from a lack and are false in nature. The very act of wanting more has its roots in not having. This lack gives birth to insecurity, fear and stress. That does not mean desire is bad. Desire is very important and in fact stimulates growth but if a desire creates stress then surely something is wrong.

On the other hand, people who don't have much are also suffering, as all they have is hope, they wonder when their desires will be fulfilled, when they will be happy. But when accomplished people are unhappy, what hope do the rest of us have? The moment one desire is fulfilled, there is another already waiting in the queue. Are you just a machine wasting your entire life in producing things and objects and rarely enjoy what is already there, your body, soul, all the gifts that nature has given and all that you have produced?

You are operating from the false centre if you feel that every action or a step forward is a struggle. If you are living like this, you will keep repeating actions that never work. This will always create a sense of anxiety and fear of failure inside you. Your mind will not be clear; there will always be some confusion and an ever-present inner conflict. You will be frustrated and feel depleted of energy. The more you struggle to get free of a problem, the more you will feel trapped.

Will you ever truly know what you really want so that you are content and peaceful? This question is relevant because each time you get what you want, you start wanting something else. This means that the happiness you get from achieving your desires is not permanent and what you get is also not what you really want. Shouldn't what you really want be fulfilling on its achievement?

Today you are not suffering because of the situations you are in or what people say to you but because you perceive these situations in the wrong way. You misinterpret what is said, what is encountered and therefore false and irrelevant feelings arise. This is false because it is not true about the present, but rather makes you see the present with a filter of the past and therefore isn't true, it isn't YOU!

Is it possible to know who creates the desire and who enjoys it? If you know this then you can create what you want rather than simply following the urge to keep on creating that which never fulfils you.

There is an old story. An emperor asked a beggar, "What do

you want?" The beggar laughed loudly and said, "You are asking me as if you can fulfil my desire!" The king was offended. He said, "I can fulfil any desire of yours. What is it, tell me. I am very powerful. What can you possibly desire that I cannot give to you?" The beggar said, "It is a simple desire. You see this begging bowl; can you fill it with something?" The king said, "Of course, I can!" He summoned one of his men and ordered him, "Fill this man's bowl with money." The man went and got some money and emptied it into the bowl, but the money disappeared. Then he poured some more and then

You can observe your thoughts; this distinguishes you from your mind and your ego.

more, and the moment he poured, it would disappear. The bowl always remained empty. Rumour spread to the whole capital and a huge crowd gathered to watch the miracle. The king's prestige was now at stake. He said to his men, "Even if the whole kingdom has to be sold, then sell it. I cannot be defeated by this beggar." His treasure chests had started to shrink. The begging bowl seemed to be bottomless. Everything that was being poured into it immediately disappeared. Finally, it was evening, and the people were standing there in utter silence when the king dropped at the feet of the beggar and admitted his defeat. He said, "Just tell me one thing. You are victorious – but before you leave, tell me, what is the begging bowl made of?" *The beggar laughed loudly and said, "There is no secret, the bowl is made from the human ego and false desires that always want more."*

The problem is that our desires are actually not ours but have been forced upon us. These desires later become the ego, which is a part of the mind. How do you distinguish this false part in you? Notice, when you say *my mind*, doesn't that mean that you are distinct and different from your mind? The mind consists of just dreams and thoughts. You can observe your thoughts; this distinguishes you from your mind and your ego. The moment you realise that the mind is separate from *you*, the mind loses its dominance over you. The unconscious, involuntary, conditioned functioning of the mind is the dominating ego and we are here to claim ourselves back from the ego's cage. This is who we are, not possessed by the mind but the one possessing it.

**Before going forward to know who you truly are,
it's important to know how the ego was created and
who you truly aren't.**

2

The Creation of the
False You: the Ego

It's very important to understand what gives birth to the ego in order to get rid of the psychological suffering that we all go through. There is bliss and focus in the absence of ego. You don't have to wait for the ego to disappear entirely, the very beginning of this process is liberating and you will start feeling confident of who you are.

You will experience psychological freedom:

- From proving yourself

- From seeking attention

- From passing judgments

- From trying to be happy

- From rushing everything you do

- From being lazy and procrastinating

- From conforming

- From emotional blocks

- From past hurts and future insecurities

We have no memories when we are born. We come to this world with an empty slate, pure and fresh. There is nothing that we know. We have no idea about the way things are and hence cannot distinguish between conditions, things, good and the bad. We are not even aware of our bodies. Slowly we become conscious and begin to recognise our own bodies. We start feeling things with the help of our parents' touch. Then we start recognising our family and the environment. We also start recognising our names. Then we start recognising our things, clothes, shoes, toys, bed, etc. We start differentiating between things as good and bad. Then we are told which religion to follow, to compete with and defeat others, think about victory all the time, look good, take care of ourselves and our family, and so on. This way our whole identity gets created and the software, the mind, keeps developing.

Our own people condition us; teachers, parents, friends, media and everybody we get in touch with, they make us absolutely selfish and self-centred as they all want us to win and defeat others. So what we presume to be our own consciousness is not ours but given to us by our surroundings and we just react like a puppet. If people appreciate us, we feel good about ourselves and since a young age our parents keep telling us how good we are and give us immense love and care. Because of this love and care that we get from everybody, we start feeling that we are significant and this forms the *I*, the *me*, the ego in us. This way we are trained to do significant and important work. We get carried away with the *I* and distance ourselves from others in trying to prove our worth. Eventually, we attach ourselves with this *I* and try becoming it all the time, all the way protecting it.

When you meet someone they are often interested only in knowing how your work is going. Due to this, our ego attributes a high level of importance to our work. Our parameter for measuring success and importance in life thus becomes money.

It is formed by the opinions of those around us, our external environment. "I" is hence a false identity, and you should not base who you are upon it, for it forms a deceptive sense of being. And this "I" goes on to become the basis of all of your misinterpretations of reality, all thought processes, interactions and relationships. Slowly and slowly your reality becomes a reflection of this false identity. Then instead of seeing reality, you only see your ego.

This formation of the ego makes us always think "me first" and others second and that's why it relates better with its own imagination, assumptions and opinions rather than on actual facts. When the ego tries to see everything through the film of its opinions, it becomes very selfish. A common complaint we hear about marriage is: "I want my way and my wife wants hers." If you observe, our wants and needs are not in conflict but it's the ego and its habit of self-centred thinking that causes trouble. If we were brought up in a different way and taught that we all are one, and that our true value lies in helping others first, we would not have had the problems we have now. Not just you, the whole world would have been a very different place.

Ego is nothing but feeling more important, different and superior to others.

Throughout life you see situations through the prism of your ego which was instilled in you when you were a child, making you who you are today. There are people who are unable to experience meaningful thoughts as they identify with

We are not living on the basis of who we are but on what we have been made to understand we should be.

them so much that they merge with their thoughts, instead of just having them. Having thoughts means you are separate from them and can see and control their unruliness. But some people associate all experiences with that one thought, that rigid conditioning and that egoistic mind. Their existence then revolves solely around the thought of defeating others, proving that they are better than others, copying others and making comparisons all the time. Your fears, too, are a result of this conditioning. A five year old who stammered while reading a chapter in front of his classmates will also stammer while giving a presentation to his clients at fifty, as he is not at ease with the source of his life. The source is in the present time but he is still stuck in the thoughts he had at age five in this particular area. So the ego is shaped by others telling us what to do and sometimes by failures that inhibit us from repeating similar mistakes. This definitely stops us from committing old mistakes again but it even stops us from doing new things, making us fear that something may go wrong.

When you attach yourself to a thought and start identifying with it, you are actually forming the ego. Then you don't have thoughts but rather you *become* your thoughts.

You are living with an ego shaped by the world outside; be it given by others or formed on the basis of your own incorrect interpretations. One who is present and aware does not allow these experiences to build in the first place, because it can ruin his life. He is always attentive and the matter is over without any images being formed in the mind that later becomes one's driving force. If one is alert and his wife gets mad at him, he will talk to her, try to find the cause behind the anger and deal with it, instead of carrying the memory of that one incident along the whole life. Then he can live with a clean slate. On the other hand, if someone tells you that the Himalayas are giant, you agree and start imagining them accordingly. But the correct way to awareness is to not form any opinions. For example, when someone tells an aware man that the new boss is rude, instead of finding evidence of his rudeness, he will find reasons to be compassionate with him. He will find the inner strength to alter his boss' actions as his egoistic energy won't be there. This way people who are aware unwittingly make others aware. We are not living on the basis of who we are but on what we have been made to understand we should be. That's why we get influenced by the world and unknowingly recreate what others are going through.

Till we find our true identity, from the awareness we have about ourselves, we will keep living someone else's life. Only self-knowledge acquired on our own can allow us independent thoughts. It's imperative to have our own thoughts and not thoughts that come from the memory given to us by others and experiences based on that. You were not born shy or a victim. You have been forming notions, that is, spinning stories right from the childhood, when you were four or five years old, based on the feedback that others gave you. You don't pay attention to the insights that you get from your own experiences due to lack of attention. You store the second-hand feelings from those experiences in the memory but not the learnings that help you grow. The ego otherwise lacks any substance and has no existence. You bring it to life and validate its existence by believing in it.

As a child, when guests come over, our parents urge us to recite poems or perform for them and the guests applaud. This is how we come to know what are we supposed to do. We find out that appreciation is good and we have to perform to earn it. This helps us grow when we are young and innocent. Ego saves us from being rejected by society when we follow what our environment has taught us. But when we follow without reasoning, all our tomorrows start springing up from our yesterdays to avoid rejection and we end up living in dejection.

The mind then begins to make rules for everything, dictating what to do and what not to do. The ego hence has images of people dictating our actions, but it also contains our self-image. The self-image has been made by the conclusions we have come to from these images. Now we don't see facts but these images ensure that our interactions are always based in the past, expecting a different future.

The ego is concerned with only our problems, creating a protective outlook while running away from the reality of the present moment. This is the survival mechanism used by the ego, protecting itself while making us suffer as it forces us to follow its dictates, doing only what it believes in. Is having an ego wrong? No, but the inability to see change, something new and unblemished, is.

Belief Makes Us Unintelligent; Images Block Our Views

There are people who believe that God exists and then there are those who don't believe in God. Those who believe, regularly chant, in their daily life if you see them they are dictators, unkind, ruthless, fraudulent and absolutely dishonest. You can find these people all around and maybe you are one of them. Can such people find God by repeating and believing certain words told by priests? These people go to the church every day but avoid acknowledging what they are: cruel and dominating. We see spiritual gurus getting jailed every other day. They are lost and think that these beliefs will clear their confusion.

We have started seeing through books and not through real experience.

So they cover up their confusion and cruelty with these beliefs. They are unable to see that beliefs are mere escape routes to avoid introspection. Beliefs are not required if one is able to see *what is* rather than only seeing *what should be*. When you are unable to see the truth, false notions are formed, making you unintelligent. Intelligence is the ability to see clearly *what is* despite your beliefs and notions.

If you pay attention, you will realise that it's this false identity that gets hurt. We say, "I am hurt." What is this "I"? From infancy we make images of ourselves in our minds. Some are made by us and many are given by other people. "I am a Muslim, I am an Indian, I am perfect," are all images. So this "I" is actually a mere image about myself that "I am an amazing man, I am very nice". This image is then damaged. One may think of oneself as a great leader, manager, husband, son or a father. These images form the interior of one's mind. When you say, "I am hurt," you actually mean that that image is hurt. If you have an image about yourself that you are perfect and your boss comes and says, "You are a moron," you get hurt. So your self-image gets hurt. The problem is now you carry that image and that hurt for the rest of your life that becomes the software, the program, of your hard drive or the brain and keep distancing yourself from your boss.

These fixed notions and thought processes that we consider to be the absolute truth slowly shape our belief system. Few beliefs and programmes are definitely useful and without them we cannot survive, but a majority become defunct with the passing of time. Most of the times when you act out of a belief, it leads to a fight as you are not willing to accept anything other than what you believe in. People around you too have their own beliefs. So one's beliefs get pitched against those of another, one's past fights with another's past and one ego fights the other. These beliefs create disbelief in many things, as one cannot see clearly through them. For example, one is hurt by one's parents emotionally; then hurt at school and college, through comparison, through rivalry, through the teacher's harsh words, etc. This hurt then continues all throughout life. Erratic actions arise from this hurt and then one builds a fortress around oneself and withdraws from relationships to avoid getting hurt again. This kind of disbelief creates fear and loneliness.

We have started seeing through books and not through real experience. For instance, while driving a car, a Hindu bow downs in front of a temple without even knowing what he is doing and the same goes for other religions as well. Whenever you try to believe in something, you are trying to work with someone else's hands, walk with someone else's legs and think with someone else's mind. Can someone else's eyes help us?

Your beliefs are evident from the labels you put on those around you. If your wife seems bossy, or your boss unfair, it's all because your interpretation is based on past experiences. The quicker you are in labelling people and situations, the farther you will be from reality. Times change, people change; we change but the notions set in our mind remain the same. They form a film through which you see life and your interpretations are hence tinted. The mind and ego keep developing with each experience till one gains control. The colour of your life is largely dependent on how coloured your beliefs are.

> **What is, is not the problem, fighting and struggling with what is, is.**

Breaking the Cage of Beliefs

I remember meeting a Buddhist monk who came to the temple situated in our house. He didn't wear any slippers and his heel was bleeding profusely. To stop the bleeding he had applied a gauze bandage that was acting like a pair of makeshift shoes. I asked the monk why he didn't wear shoes because the bandage is acting like a shoe only and he could easily buy shoes made out of cloth. He said Buddhist religious text does not mention shoes. I told him, "You get the text; I will write in it, will you wear them then?"

What this saint does not realise is that he is actually a programmed robot, reacting to 5000-year-old commands, which have now become his belief. Buddha said not to wear shoes during those times as they were made out of animal leather back then but now shoes are available in all materials, like rubber, plastic, synthetic and cloth, where no harm to animals is caused while making them. Earlier it was okay to not wear shoes as there were roads made of soft mud but now they are hard-surfaced and cause harm to their feet. Instead of learning from your own experiences, you look at others. Our system of understanding is getting defunct as we have not let it develop because of conforming, imitating and following others as it is hard work to find your own ways. Our feelings now choose the easier way of following others. People say one should eat on time, now if someday you don't feel like eating on time, you will still eat and your health may deteriorate because of it. You are not aware of your own feelings but guided by your conditioning and that's why everything has become topsy-turvy today.

The good thing about belief is that a person who believes that he is responsible for his life will view challenges in a very different way than one who is at the mercy of others and situations. The belief that you and only you are responsible for what you make of a given situation is the right kind of belief. Life does not happen to you but is a result of how you respond to opportunities and challenges. The problem arises when belief occupies the driver's seat and takes control, not allowing you to operate with a clear mind and awareness from the present moment requirements. Beliefs then imprison you, making you aggressive and egocentric. You start living in a world dominated by your beliefs, as imagined by your ego, you resist and reject the truth that is right in front of you. The ego looks for what is in your mind, what you believe in. It binds us and makes us slaves.

Creation of My Ego

When you read my story, please don't get sucked into it, keep in mind your own story. Have you wondered why many of us have a hard time dealing with relationships, settling in our careers and living peacefully? It's time to check some deep-rooted emotions that block the flow of mental energy essential to have the right perception, and choosing the right action, in the right direction.

I am the grandson of Late Shri Shankarlalji S. Kasliwal, Founder Chairman, S. Kumars, and later I became Kumar Mangalam Birla's brother-in-law as my first cousin, Neerja *jiji*, married him. I was born into a rich family. My father was an honest, charismatic man. He was one of the founder-directors in the illustrious S. Kumars group and son of the chairman. He was the first in the group to set up an industry at Indore, establishing Pankaj Tyres in 1968, when he was just 24 years old. He was the life of the house and great to be around because of his magnetic personality. He was cherished by his family and friends. Everyone wanted to be around him and I too admired his qualities. But he was inclined towards spirituality. Gradually he renounced the material world, after starting a few more ventures, and embraced the spiritual world fully. After he stepped down from his coveted designation, a mere illusion of affluence was left to us. This made me unknowingly ostentatious in my way of living, especially in front of my own people, family and friends. You have to show off something only when you don't have it. Many relatives distanced themselves from us; perhaps what kept them glued to us earlier was money and not the bond of blood. My father handled the situation with strength and resilience, accepting it as his destiny, and embraced spirituality. He sprang back stronger and dealt with situations using his inner power and intuition.

During my initial struggle what kept me alive was my father's voice and wisdom. I learnt to live on mere words. He would still talk about opening a public limited company with people who would come to meet him. Some of my friends would laugh at him after hearing his ideas. They saw a family that didn't even have a proper car or decent means to live, and a man who, they felt, continued to brag. They also mistook his righteousness for an inflated ego and aggression. But I could relate to him, his spirit and passion, and continued to have trust and faith in him as he did all that to keep us buoyant. Despite not having much money, he enrolled all us siblings, three brothers and a sister, in the best school, The Daly College, Indore. Most parents don't even have the courage to send their children to ordinary schools after going through such trying circumstances. My mother sold all her jewellery to bring us up.

In the midst of all this, our father gave us a fantastic upbringing as he had seen the best of both worlds. He was an industrialist and problems had taught him to deal with life intelligently. We never had money in our pocket because after his stepping down from S. Kumars he couldn't establish himself again. One of my friends would joke, saying, "Our parents ensure that we take money before leaving and Shashank's parents ensure that he doesn't carry any." Initially, when I went out with friends, I would often not eat as I never had the money to contribute. Still I would go without a sign of remorse and just keep drinking water. This made me confident and I gained courage, making a resolve to go anywhere without money and still have fun. My father never formally taught us to speak the truth but I learnt from him as he demonstrated these universal laws by living them.

However, my attention-seeking behaviour and habit of showing off soon turned problematic. I started comparing myself to others. I convinced myself that one can be happy without money and yet I experienced that no one actually respects you if you don't have a big car and a big bungalow to boast of, barring a few friends and family members. An inner conflict began to develop. I felt confident even without money but on the other hand was failing repeatedly in establishing a stable business, which further lowered my spirits. Society lays great emphasis on success and everybody started asking me why my business failed despite all my positivity.

I was very diligent while handling my life and dealing with real-time situations as I had faced so many of them. Self-awareness led me to the right solutions and honed my perception and intuition, helping me deal with life. Today I train corporate executives, managers, senior managers and workers on deconditioning, working and living happily, producing optimal results in life and inspire people to carry on living with inner power, irrespective of their financial conditions. All these tough times I handled with just one line from my father in mind, "Keep doing your best, respect others and help as much as you can." It worked but the journey was long and arduous.

Egoistic Strengths Give Different Results

I experienced that the strengths that helped me succeed at times also became my greatest barriers while moving forward in life. My father would always say, "You are powerful even without money because a majority of the people hesitate and lose because they lack faith." We definitely didn't have the money but had immense faith in ourselves and in our ability to create it unlike those who despite having money lacked faith. I had learned to live without money but the flip side was that earning money took a back seat. I became comfortable living with less money and instead of putting in efforts in planning and focusing, I started becoming spiritual. I was always hardworking, but I lacked focus. I learnt that proving myself to a client earned me business but while proving myself in front of friends, I lost them.

Howsoever your upbringing may be, you cannot escape conditioning. It works both ways; the same set of beliefs lead to results but also hinder us in other areas. Before becoming a trainer and an author I had to go through the ordeal of learning to be intrinsically powerful. I got a variety of exposure. My father had a textile mill, a tyre manufacturing set up and a plastic unit, all of which gave me the exposure and business acumen required to start a variety of my own ventures such as exporting leather toys, setting up a fitness centre, launching a newspaper, packaging mineral water, manufacturing sanitary ware and doing various odd jobs in colleges for almost seven years. None of these ventures worked and the jobs too didn't click. My identity became the foundation for my career as a trainer. Professionally my ego made me one of the best corporate trainers wherever I worked but also the worst friend, as I would try to solve the problems of my friends without them even asking.

For my real education, I studied myself. I learnt what *knowing* is, not intellectually, but at the level of the very fibre, muscle and bone of my body. I started contemplating how life works and how to get up when down, not just once, but umpteen numbers of times. You should know when to go to the doctor and when to handle things yourself using your inner knowledge. One small example is not popping pills for headaches but relaxing and resting.

Formation of Emotional Blocks

My parents and I went to the US when I was just six months old. When we came back to India I started school, where I had a tough time making friends. Somewhere from my environment, my family and cousins, I had picked up arrogance at that young age and maybe brought along some from my past karmas as well. As a result, I was very flamboyant and bossy. At home I was treated with love but in junior school nobody played with me as I was dominating and was too young to recognize the same. I started feeling rejected and developed a victim complex. Instead of handling issues, I focused on their effect on me, that is the moods and irritation that came along with the inability to figure out a solution. As a result, my classmates began avoiding me. To get their attention I would do all kinds of things, an extreme example being throwing sweets in the air and making them run after them. They would take the sweets but still avoid me. I regularly acted in ways that made it hard for other kids to accept me. Somewhere this urge to prove myself also made me a good sportsman. I excelled in sports, became the school athletics team's captain and later became a national athlete. Even though I knew how good I was, I kept trying to prove myself because I didn't feel accepted. My feelings made me feel suppressed and repressed, a victim of my circumstances, and that later turned into depression, despite having the best upbringing. Though I eventually realised that those small kids who are great friends now didn't even know what I was going through at that time. They were not mature enough to deal with a bully and I wasn't mature enough to understand that I was bullying them. It wasn't the real me but my acquired personality that made me act out in order to get something.

Because of the rejection I faced in my formative years at school, I developed a hostile behaviour and an egoistic personality that further kept fellow students away from me. I could understand what rejection was only after being rejected. One has to drown to learn to swim. I was getting better and better at handling situations and my emotional upheavals but continued to struggle with people. So when I saw somebody doing something wrong, I would upset people by lecturing and confronting them. And nobody wants to stay with someone who is so upright that they feel threatened in his company. Arrogance puts you at the centre of your world and you end up ignoring other people's needs. It continues to justify your behaviour, not listening and understanding those around you.

Some of these early childhood memories prevailed, affecting

me even in later classes, so I couldn't connect even with the few classmates who tried to approach me, barring a few girls. I always missed that heart-to-heart connection with boys. In spite of some very good friendships, I always felt left out, which kept draining me. However, things changed when new students joined after the 10th standard and they saw me, without the shadow of my past looming above, they saw me as I was. I had great friends after this, but developed a very invulnerable and defensive personality. Such defence mechanisms tend to remain in place even when the child becomes an adult until and unless one makes conscious efforts to get past it. Despite having friends, I was still conditioned to show off and seek attention all the time. I developed an acidic tongue and indulged in sharp repartees to appear witty and attract people's attention. People would often find it difficult to deal with me and didn't accept me. On top of this, I would misinterpret things and try to find clues of people's dislike for me, even where none existed. I developed a huge emotional block. My ego was the product of my environment but it wasn't me. I developed an ego that doesn't actually exist. It was all in my head, it had no substance. I gave it life by believing in it.

The ego is false and exists only because you don't know yourself and operate upon the external stimulus. Is there a YOU that is separate from your thoughts, feelings, and reactions? Or are these emotions felt by nobody, just a movement without a centre? The moment you see yourself at the centre, this ego disappears.

The False Content of My Ego – *I Became Who I Am and Also Who I Am Not*

I was complicated, disciplined, confident, street-smart, egoistic, sweet, straight-talking, honest and a nice guy. But I was also ostentatious, pretended to be rich and didn't put in enough effort in earning till I became aware of everything false inside of me. My false identity, the ego, made me judgmental, reactive, comparing, competitive, suppressed, repressed and stuck in my comfort zones, the outcomes were restlessness and fear that led me to clamp up internally, only expressing myself through anger and bouts of sadness that only I knew about.

Changing Fails

To change my identity I used means like partying and travelling; others use alcohol and other toxic substances. I was constantly trying to impress people, be smart, witty, humorous and kind all the time. Do we do all this to try to impress others or impress ourselves? Being smart is not bad by itself, but it is when done to impress others. My ego urged me to always be what I learnt from my father, to be always laughing, boasting irrespective of the actual conditions. Pretending to be something that I was not, I assumed his reality to be mine. He was not pretending but I was. I found that I was neither like my father nor the altered identity. Neither of the two was truly me. And because of these false identities I kept on failing in life and the effort of proving myself was draining my energy.

When my business ventures failed, I started looking for a job in Delhi. I would simply dash into anyone's office and once even entered B M Munjal's (Hero MotoCorp Limited's owner) cabin and asked for a job. I didn't know whom to turn to. Mr. Munjal applauded my confidence and recognized my surname, 'Kasliwal', as he knew my uncles. Though I didn't get a job, I realised that having confidence in yourself is not the same as having what it takes to succeed. I learnt that confidence is not a personality trait or sheer flamboyance; it is the correct assessment of a situation that sparks motivation. If you have confidence, you are motivated to put in effort, invest time and resources, and persist in reaching the goal. It's not confidence itself that results in success, it's the investment and effort that you put in. Without enough confidence, it's too easy to give up prematurely or not get started at all. Hopelessness and despair prevent positive action. I realised that because of my ego I was just showing off and not putting in the right effort and this was making me unhappy. However, I used my unhappiness as it showed me the way. It helped me realise that this is not who I am. I cannot stay stressed and try to escape the reality by drinking, partying irresponsibly and resorting to other such means, I had to find the real me.

Sometimes you need a jolt, a sharp blow to get out of your slumber and find the real you. I realised my true self when I started developing illnesses that accompany the stress and inner conflict of trying to be someone you are not. I developed thyroid and tinnitus and because of the unease caused by these I learnt what I wasn't. People's responses to my behaviour were another clue that made me look within. Finding my real self-made me realise that we can have fun all the time when we are psychologically free, work and live in a 'pull environment' and not push to get things done. When you live as your true self, you pull; attract what is needed. The struggle disappears and effortless efforts flow. Then there is no scope for insecurity as you are secure in the way you live, fully aware, when there is clarity and no stress.

3

Consciousness – the Real You

What is consciousness? The one who is behind your body, behind your thoughts is the one we are talking about. The real you, the source and generator of true happiness, an inner stillness that you can feel from the inside, is different from the egoistic mind. When you become present to this inner presence, you are aware, alert, awake and have attention. When you lose inner stillness, you lose contact with yourself. Your innermost sense of self, sense of who you are is the presence of stillness. This presence is who you are which goes deeper than your body, name and fame. Throughout this book, our intention is to know this presence, which is your true nature.

If you observe the inner working of your own mind carefully, you will be able to see that there is no experience of the present as your thoughts are always shuffling between the past and the future. Our ego tries to escape facing the present by either living in the past or creating hopes for the future.

Consciousness is a person's awareness towards his ego's activities and the functioning of his own mind. It is the state of being aware of and responsive to one's surroundings rather than reacting to everything based on preconceived notions. So, you can make anything real. You can make a temple out of stones or you can respect your parents as gods. It all depends on your consciousness. Where you are really conscious is *your* world.

When you experience consciousness, you start feeling fresh. It is that state of pure awareness which allows you to feel wakefulness, instils in you a sense of pristine selfhood, and grants you full access to the executive control system of the mind. Anything that we are aware of at a given moment forms part of our consciousness. It is therefore filled with content. The content consists of the way you think, the way you live, the way you believe, the way you react,

Ego forms when there is identification with these thoughts.

your behaviour, your ego and everything that is a part of your life. In essence, poverty, worry, insecurity, confusion, emotional wounds and fear of any kind also is content and becomes the consciousness which is you. This content – the way you think and act – has been taught to you by the society, parents, education and learnt from your own insufficient experiences. Our reality is not what the society has made us into as this content divides us and we stay split within. It's always something of me and something of the society.

Thinking: Noise in the Head

Being aware of the consciousness is realising that your identity is not what your thinking says it is. The noise that fills your head is not who you are. Thinking without awareness is the biggest problem of our existence. Consciousness makes it possible for me to see that I am separate from the thought. Ego forms when there is identification with these thoughts. Consciousness is when you understand that unconscious thinking will lead to a repeat of past experiences and only perpetuate pain. Present to this fact is being aware and in the realm of the consciousness.

Ego leads you to be absent as you don't know how to stay present. Many people can't even experience the weather. If they have experienced a slight chill yesterday, they feel cold even the day after as they are not aware. The moment you know yourself, that is, you know your consciousness, the ego automatically disappears. Consciousness is your inner nature that is available in the present moment, going the way life naturally takes you and not trying to change things psychologically on the dictates of the ego. It means being alive in the moment and aware of the movement of your thoughts. When you are aware of the movement of your thoughts, they stop on their own and you can see things with clarity in the present. When the ego disappears, what is left is consciousness. Consciousness is the one who observes everything when it is not attached to the ego. When it is attached to the ego, it thinks, feels, imagines and goes through what the ego makes it go through, thus losing its identity. The whole idea of this book is to give you tremendous confidence and enthusiasm by shifting this consciousness away from the domain of the ego, emotions, thinking, past hurts, sorrows and pain.

You will remain a liar, albeit unknowingly, if you lose yourself in the preoccupations of the ego as you don't know the truth about yourself. If you don't go to a party, the ego will say, you should have. If you go, you feel bored. You will always hate others, expecting love from them, not realising that the source of love lies in your own self. You will hate others because you are judging them on all the wrong parameters; you will hate life as the one who is seeing all this is itself a false entity. You cannot be considerate and feel for others as all your feelings are created by something that you are not. This way we end up unknowingly pretending. As long as you continue to operate

When the ego disappears, what is left is consciousness.

from the ego, you can only pretend, you can put in the effort but everything will remain superficial and only skin-deep. That's why, notice, the moment someone interrupts what we're saying or breaks our expectations and even the smallest of unpleasant situations bring out the animal that is hidden in us. Our vengeful instincts get activated. I say active because they are always lying there, dormant, because you are not what you are. That's why you need to notice the repression inside of you. Leading a life of repression is to live a life that you were not meant to live, to do things that you never wanted to do, to be a person you are not, it's a way to destroy yourself. Expression is life; repression is suicide.

Are You in the Right Place?

Majority of us are trying to be what we are not, and therefore heading to all the wrong places. No wonder the condition of the world is such. No one is in the right place. The doctor actually wanted to be an engineer, the photographer tried to be a teacher, the businessman tried to hold on to a job, so on and so forth. This is the true cause of inner suffering; we are trying to become someone else rather than just being who we truly are. Almost everybody is tensed, because all actions are coming from the ego and there is always a conflict due to indecisiveness. Your consciousness goes in one direction; your ego goes in the exact opposite direction, making you divided inside. A divided, split personality cannot be happy or energetic. Many of us are somehow pulling ourselves together; sometimes with the help of alcohol, sometimes with foreign trips (if we can afford them), always trying to seek attention and appreciation, trying to avoid reality. Are you one of those who is just trying to be rich, famous and slim because that's what's going to give you the grit to face the world? We have seen many across the world hunt and kill innocent animals in order to feel powerful. In real life, these people get hunted every day with mere words. If they would just realise the innocence of these animals, they could become receptive to other people, their suffering and reactive minds too.

As you start becoming conscious of the unconsciousness, you experience greater calm within as you start listening to yourself, your instincts, your feelings, your intelligence and do not run away hunting others for their mistakes. You start depending on yourself, going wherever spontaneity takes you. A feeling of balance takes over and your actions turn into appropriate responses to the present moment rather than being mere reactions and repetitions of past mistakes. Happiness does not require effort; it comes effortlessly when you follow your nature and be yourself. There is nothing to be obtained or attained in order for one to be happy and no struggle is required to attain it either.

Unhappiness, on the other hand, is a constant state for many as they try so hard to be happy and it only aggravates the problems. The ego has pre-set ideas about what is right and what is wrong. Happiness and peace cannot be achieved by such ready-made ideas. Their ideas don't work because life goes on changing and the ego remains rigid and unchanged. You always find yourself unfit, because if you follow your ego, you have to go against the current of life; if you follow life, you have to go against your ego. That's why the whole effort has to be put in for being conscious and that will give rise to spontaneity. You go prepared to say something to your wife but when you reach she says something to you that you are not prepared to handle. When you are aware and alert you respond to people and situations on the basis of the present, ensuring that whatever you do is right. It is not a question of actions being right or wrong, it is a question of consciousness – whether you are doing it consciously or unconsciously in the grip of your ego, like a robot. All actions coming out of the ego are unconscious.

Unconscious Actions

One fine day, a bus driver went to the garage, started his bus and drove along the route. No problems for the first few stops, a few people got on, a few got off, and things went well. At the next stop, however, a big hulk got on – six feet eight, built like a wrestler, arms hanging down to the ground. He glared at the driver and said, "Big John doesn't pay!" and sat down at the back. Naturally, the driver didn't argue with Big John, but he wasn't happy about it.

The next day the same thing happened – Big John got on again, made a show of refusing to pay and sat down and the next day, and the one after that, and so forth. This grated on the bus driver, who started losing sleep over the way Big John was taking advantage of him. Finally, he could stand it no longer. He signed up for defence and martial arts courses: karate, judo, and all the good stuff. By the end of the summer he had become quite strong, and what's more, he felt really good about himself.

So the next Monday, when Big John once again got on the bus and said, "Big John doesn't pay!" the driver stood up, glared back at him, and screamed, "And why not?" With a surprised look on his face, Big John replied, "Because Big John has a bus pass."

Previously, the bus driver's his ego reacted on seeing the big man. This is what we are all doing; whether it's a challenge or an opportunity, we stay glued to our own notions and react to the past instead of being attentive in the present. Awareness is always there, whether you are aware towards the ego, that is your thoughts, you are identified with, or your consciousness. When you are aware of the consciousness, the thoughts are not there which allows you to be present in the moment.

**Look where you are going or you will
go where you are looking.**

We are using the word consciousness in the context of ATTENTION, the witnessing presence that is AWARE without judging or evaluating and that which sees the working of the ego. Here it is used as a separate entity and is not a part of the ego. When this consciousness is present, we call it the 'presence of the presence'.

Understanding Consciousness as Attention

I am reminded of an old story about a businessman: he was getting old and had a daughter. He told his daughter, "To succeed in life, one has to learn the art of dropping the ego. This will make you a good human being and a successful businesswoman, too. To learn this art, I am sending you to a master archer." The daughter got a little confused and thought, *what has archery to do with being a good businesswoman?* But on her father's advice, she decided to go visit the master. She was pleased to see the old master who was incredibly peaceful and was surrounded by an aura of grace. His very presence was making her calm. The daughter touched his feet and said, "Meeting you, now all my confusion is gone and I am in a hurry to learn the art." The master said, "Sorry young girl, nothing can be learnt in a rush. Infinite patience is the base of learning, and this is your first and primary lesson.

"For the next lesson, you will be doing odd jobs, cleaning the entire ashram, maintaining the gardens, throwing away old leaves and fruits… The learning will happen; I may come and strike you with a thick wooden stick at any time." The daughter was willing but amazed and amused at this new way of training and asked, "Are you sure this will help me in becoming a good businesswoman, not break my bones?" "You will come to know as time passes by," said the old man. She was an intelligent girl but was still puzzled as to how someone can learn anything by getting beaten up.

The time came and when she started cleaning, the master started hitting her. She would be collecting fruits in the garden and a strike would land. She would be washing the ceiling and all of a sudden a smack would distract her from cleaning. She would be removing stones from the ashram's path and a smack out of the blue would come her way. The master was peaceful but his ways were making her jittery. But she began to learn and was surprised. Within a few days she developed a certain insight, an intuition. She experienced, as the master approached her, she would jump out of his way like a spring. After a few days, irrespective of what she was doing, some part of her consciousness was alert all the time and aware of where the master was. The master was a veteran and used to walk very silently, making it almost impossible for anyone to hear him approach. But she started being conscious after her whole body hurt with the pain caused by the beatings.

This continued for over a month. But in just one month she became so able that the master was no longer able to hit her. The master said, "You really are the daughter of your father. He too was very dedicated. Your first lesson is over today because, for the past 24 hours I've been trying to hit you, but you have always been alert and managed to save yourself.

"From tomorrow morning, instead of a wooden stick, there will be a double-edged iron sword. The stick that we used earlier may have given you swellings but this can hack you to death, so more consciousness will be required."

The young girl had learnt so much in her first month about the levels of intuition and insightful consciousness possible, it made her more courageous. She was not at all afraid even of the iron sword. She accepted and said, "It is going to be the same, just like I could protect myself from the wooden stick, I will be able to save myself from this real sword too. I am starting to understand what you are trying to teach me so it doesn't make any difference to me."

The training started and the master tried hitting her in every way possible but the girl became more and more alert. She had to, there was no choice. The master could not touch her even once and another month elapsed. The master was really satisfied and was encouraged to give her the final lesson. But when he revealed what the final lesson was, she was shocked. He said, "Till now I was trying to hit you while you were awake but from today evening, I may hit you even when you are asleep. This will start again with the wooden stick that we used initially."

Worry gripped the girl because evading the master's beatings was easier when awake, but how can one be aware while asleep? But two months had made her respect the master and she had immense trust in his skills. She felt innately confident about her own intuition. So she thought *if the master says so then maybe consciousness, awareness and intuition are always awake, they never sleep.* She started getting the gist of the lesson – the mind sleeps, the body sleeps, but the consciousness is always awake. *The basic nature of consciousness is attention and awareness but people never think about it that way.* So she thought *I should experience it. I should be alert, even when I am asleep.*

The master started striking her, and a few times she even got hurt very badly. But she felt grateful and not angry at all, because with each strike, she grew more alert, even while sleeping. She experienced consciousness as a flame that remained alive, alert and watchful within her. Just after one month she was able to save herself even in her sleep. She was amazed at her awareness, as the master would come nearby, very silently, making no noise, and yet the young girl would jump out of the bed. Many a times, she would be fast asleep but something in her remained alert and awake.

Next morning when the master was sitting in the sun, reading the *Gita*, a thought came to the young girl's mind, *this master, who is quite old, has been really hitting me, it will be a good idea to hit him and test his alertness.* She went towards him and as she thought of hitting him, from just thirty feet away, the master said, "Girl, I am very old, and your training is not complete yet, so don't entertain such foolish ideas."

The girl could not believe it. She touched the master's feet and said, "Sorry, please forgive me, I have not done anything, it was just an idea." The master said, "Consciousness makes you so alert even your thoughts can be heard. It is all about awareness. You think and the master will know; you don't have to do anything. With little more patience, soon you too will become equally awake."

The next day again the master was sitting in the sun and reading the *Gita*, the girl sensed a thought so clearly that she went to the master, and said, "You are going to strike me again?" The master said, "You are absolutely right, I was just thinking about coming over after completing this page. Now your training is over, you don't need to be here." The young girl said, "What about being a good businesswoman?" The master said, "Forget all about it. A girl who is so alert can only be good, pure and free from the ego's occupations. She cannot harm anybody, she cannot steal, she cannot be unkind or cruel; she will be naturally loving and compassionate. You forget all about the ego and be good now!"

This is consciousness. The girl returned home. Her father was waiting and he asked, "So, have you mastered the art of archery?" The young girl said, "Where did you get the idea of teaching me archery?" The father said, "I had sent you to learn wakefulness and consciousness, archery was only a medium."

When consciousness dawns on you, you start helping others as you are present in the moment and don't operate from the false ego that only thinks about itself. People will not be able to fool you with words as you would have the capability to see through their words, their intentions, their true feelings, the meaning and the context. The content will be more or less irrelevant. The moment consciousness disassociates itself from the ego you are activated and there is a gush of energy and enthusiasm. This way, you will be able to use your mind when needed and not get used by it because of its unconscious ways of functioning.

Knowing Consciousness

Many people move through life as if they're sleepwalking, not at all present to what they are doing, why they are doing it, never alert to their surroundings, not even aware of what motivates them, not aware of the things they say and do. The real problem is that you see yourself through your ego and keep doing what you don't want to do, you go on doing things that you have decided not to do, doing things you know are wrong and you don't do things that you know are right.

The ego makes you think that you are your achievements, your money, your behaviour, your thinking, the attention you get and everything else but it doesn't let you see the one who experiences all this, the consciousness. You keep seeing what you think and lose the capability to *be yourself.*

4

Mechanics behind Working of the Ego

This chapter will help us see the mechanics of the ego so that we can handle it with ease. The ego comes into existence through identification; whatever you identify with turns into ego. When you are attached to something and that something gets lost, you suffer. Your pen is misplaced, you suffer. As a child, you suffered when you lost your toy. The objects change over time but the suffering remains the same. It is not the loss, but the attachment you have to the object that causes the suffering. The thoughts of *me, mine, more than, I want, I need, I must have,* and *not enough* form the backbone of the ego.

The object keeps changing but the backbone remains the same.

There was a man whose car caught fire. He started crying and shouting and in the midst of all this his son came running, "Father don't worry, I had just sold the car half an hour back to our far away uncle". The father started laughing and thanked his luck. Just a minute ago he was howling. During all this, the uncle to whom the son had sold the car came over. He said, "I am not going to pay for the burnt car. Now there's just a burning car, which will turn to ashes in a few minutes". The father started crying again. Notice what happened, this very understanding can free you from the ego right away. When he heard that the car was sold, he relaxed even though the car was still burning. But when he came to know that the uncle won't pay, he began crying again. So the attachment is not with the car but with *my* car. The pain results from the feeling of *my* and not from the object itself, otherwise he would have cried for the car even though it was sold.

Beyond the object, we are attached to being accepted, understood, respected, liked, needed, valued, being in control, right, treated fairly, getting attention, feeling included, enjoying freedom, achieving peacefulness, and having balance, consistency, order, comfort, variety, love, safety, predictability, fun, new challenges and autonomy. All these are created through our experiences, exposure and upbringing.

Ego makes life miserable with all these attachments. An unattached approach enables you to simply enjoy life; it makes you responsive, aware of positive things, enthusiastic and full of vitality as one is free from the fear of losing which comes from attachments. Detachment means being free from the feeling of *my*, being unconditional in what you do, what you seek, what you love and what you experience. Nothing has to be changed to be unattached; it's just the approach that needs to be channelized.

Don't give up desires for things or relationships, but rather:

- Give up your attachment to them

- Remain untouched by them

If you look at your relationships, you will notice that they are more of an obsession with each other, giving a sense of possessiveness. This possessiveness makes us impose ourselves on the other. Therefore, one should understand the implication, its requirements and why we get attached to anything. Look deeply, when you are attached to a thing or a person, there is always an element of fright in it, the anxiety of losing something. There is always a sense of fear and insecurity. There is always the anxiety of separation. For example, I am attached to my job. I am attached to it because it satisfies my survival needs, gives me enjoyment and fulfilment. My attachment also makes me envious of all other colleagues and scared of losing my position. Where there is envy, there is extreme dislike, too. So see for yourself, do you actually love your job, your people, or are you just attached to them?

The problem with possessing things is that we become what we possess. The man who identifies himself with his car limits his existence to the car, or his mobile phone or his mansion, and the same applies to point of views, or with individuals. Notice, when one is possessive, the love is lost and one loses the essence of relationships, too. Is that why we try to gather things and people and possessions because we are hollow and empty from the inside? So we try to fill the void with our possessions because we are empty from the inside? We fill it with alcohol, people, entertainment, enjoyment, knowledge, music, etc., trying to be content. Is this really a life you want for yourself? You get attached and if anything is missing you are sad because it makes you realise your inner emptiness.

You can stay unattached to your relationships, actions and experiences when you start being conscious and attentive to your ego and how it triggers you to act. If you think about the suffering all of us go through because of the ego, you will find that being present and staying unattached is very easy to practice. Wherever there is psychological pain, the ego isn't far behind. You getting angry, comparing yourself, feeling jealous, reacting and projecting your perceptions on others are all results of psychological suffering. We often fail to take note of this; we are used to treating physical pain by going to the doctor, but psychologically we have become so used to suffering that we assume that is how life is. But when you start becoming aware of your sufferings, you by default will start taking corrective action, which will be elaborated upon in the techniques section of this book.

But before that, take this for instance: your boss gives you a project. Now before starting to work, ordinarily we figure out that upon completing the project, we will be appreciated, respected and maybe even given a promotion. This is the attached approach through which the ego works. In the unattached approach, you get on with the work without thinking about rewards and instead think about how you can give the project your best by being focused in the present. This frees up your energy, making sure that they are used to spot creative ideas, take suggestions and give you the courage required to take the right decisions. There is space in the mind as it is no longer cluttered with expectations. When you work in an unattached approach, your ego drops that which keeps you self-centred, making your attention, which is instrumental to completing work with perfection, increase manifold.

Working and living with this approach not only makes your work outstanding but also lets you realise your purpose of living, which is to enjoy life in everything you do. You experience freedom as your happiness is not dependent on anything. You enjoy the very experience of life itself. Each situation then is an experience, even when things don't go your way. Ego functions on the basis of boundaries, a self-centred approach, and the resulting choices. The unattached approach comes from consciousness and thus it is tantamount to alertness. Because of alertness without the compulsion to choose, one is able to enjoy 'free will' even if limitations are imposed, as the enjoyment of bliss is no longer dependent on any particular outcome. Being conscious leads to bliss as you are fully present to life and that makes you compassionate towards other people.

Ego never lets you be compassionate with people and therefore there is no scope left for clarity of purpose. But when you are unattached, you have the opportunity to be yourself as there is no fear. Compassion helps in creating healthy relationships whereas the ego keeps you burdened with memories of the past (who did what to you) and you get stuck in the uncertainties of the future.

The compassion we are talking about is not an emotionless repetition of being civil and kind. The ego and the mind are always caught in directionless, selfish thinking and so cannot be compassionate at all. Compassion is action taken without the intention of getting something in return. Such compassion frees the mind of its negativity and operates from a very different kind of intelligence to see the purpose of life in comparison to the shrewd intelligence of the ego. You may be very smart in your academics, in your work or debating with people rationally but that is not the intelligence that will give you an insight into a meaningful life.

Intelligence goes with love and compassion as they are present where the consciousness is and the ego isn't. When such intelligence is present, the difference between you and other people vanishes, which opens up *The problem arises when instead of using material things, you start getting used by them, trying to prolong the satisfaction. The ego becomes dependent on them for constructing your identity.* the purpose of life. This purpose of life is not only for you but for all living beings.

Then you won't help people to get something in return, but because they need it. Their needs then become yours. Their pain becomes yours. This further enlightens you regarding the goals of your soul. Once your confusion is gone, you have ample energy to think, plan and act with awareness.

The ego's mechanism can be beaten when one realises this and does not look far ahead out of sheer anxiety or obsessively plan things in advance to feel secure. Such actions will be free of confusion. There won't be wasteful repetitive thinking and procrastination. A man of action lives without fear. He is content with what life offers to him and accepts life as it comes without complaints. All his goals are fulfilled, as he is contented from the inside which is the purpose of life. Contentment gives clarity and such a man enjoys the riches of the worldly pursuits and is capable of doing the right action.

Planning is important but thinking about it all the time is not helpful. The ego has the tendency to live in the thoughts about the plan and inevitably hamper the action by draining all the energy in thinking about the plan.

Ego weighs you down and doesn't let you be a carefree traveller in the journey of self-discovery. You can travel towards self-discovery only with complete trust in the present moment. Once you awaken your consciousness, you will not just think about objects but work for what you want in the material world without psychologically suffering from insecurity and fear.

Self-Hypnosis

When you keep repeating the same thought over and over again, you are actually hypnotising yourself. When you look at something for a long time you get attached to it and a desire arises to possess it.

This is exactly how the ego works. When you keep looking at something, it could even be a thought that is stuck in your head, the mind assumes that this is your interest and formulates a plan to achieve it. This planning is not necessarily logical; in fact, it is emotional, because how the ego operates is through attachment. You get attached to something if you experience emotions related to it. No emotion means no attachment and no attachment means you are free of emotion.

Working of the Ego in Action

- Ego wants you to stand out from the crowd.

- Ego is attached to your physical appearance.

- Ego makes you want different things, not what you have in the present.

- Ego feeds on things that make you feel superior to others.

- Ego makes you feel inferior when others have more than you or better things than you.

- Ego makes you want to appear happy, attractive and youthful only superficially.

- Ego tries to be exclusive by possessing expensive things and associating with those it considers powerful, just to feel unique.

- Ego doesn't let you accept anybody else's triumphs, it makes you feel small.

- Ego always makes you someone you're not.

- Ego easily gets hurt as it has almost zero tolerance.

- Ego makes you judgmental and attention-seeking.

The Ego Always Wants More

You will have noticed that the satisfaction derived from the ego is very short-lived, so you keep looking for more, keep buying, consuming, wandering and pretending. The problem arises when instead of using material things, you start getting used by them, trying to prolong the satisfaction. The ego becomes dependent on them for constructing your identity. More than actually having things, the ego is attached to wanting things because it is a false identity created psychologically. That's why its fulfilment lies not in having but in wanting. Oblivious to this, we keep running after what the ego tells us to. Notice how people keep sharing their plans, they might not have achieved anything but they keep talking about what they are going to achieve in the future. The ego even sells unrealised desires to buy satisfaction for you.

It is in our hands, however, to just keep playing our best shot. Just keep doing the right thing, work with authenticity and commitment, work hard and enjoy it. To continue its dominance, the ego keeps asking for more. It is good to work more but don't make it conditional to living. The more you want things, the less you get them because the desire itself comes in the way of fulfilment. Often there are unfulfilled desires that lead to frustration and welled-up anger, forming an obstacle that blocks your happiness. By default your confidence to achieve goes down and you start feeling that desire for objects is the cause of unhappiness. But it is not so. It is the ego that makes us suffer. The *I* is the hidden culprit. The best part is, it is within us and in our control and we need not try changing others or our circumstances.

Ego dies the moment you stop wanting.

Understanding Desire

As the *Bhagavad Gita* says, and we ourselves experience, we are being pulled into so many desires all the time. This splits us from the inside and our consciousness, that is the centre, gets lost in the desires, creating emotional clutter. The problem is, we are unable to distinguish between the desires of the mind and desire as energy.

The mind has definitely given us lot of progress outwards but at the same time robbed us completely on the inside. The mind desires objects because that's the way it has been conditioned: a big car, a better house, a beautiful wife, good clothes, foreign trips, a great job, respect, etc. All this is important and one should definitely work towards raising the quality of life. Yet, somewhere, something is going wrong and that's why many people who have achieved all this still look dissatisfied and discontented. If you observe, those who have all the riches have become comfortable physically but the deeper problems of their minds remain the same and they continue to suffer. They still feel insecure when someone doesn't invite them to an event, they still compare themselves to people richer than them, they still fear all the 'what if' thoughts and they also have the added tension of losing what they have earned, they have issues trusting people when people come asking for help as they feel that the whole world wants to take away their money. If you observe and genuinely ask yourself whether the money has made any difference, you'll easily realise that rich people have become more angry, restless and disturbed than before. That does not mean that earning money is bad but thinking that money will handle your psychological issues is like asking a fish to fly.

Desire is Energy

Actually, when there is no attachment to objects, goals, ideas, opinions and people, what remains is the pure energy of desire. This energy is our life force and needs to be protected from the ego, the *I* that is conditioned to gather objects, respect, attention, importance and making itself significant all the time.

The idea is not to be afraid of desire but to channelize it from objects to expanding consciousness.

Our desire for objects is just the façade, a cover up of our real needs. One who is running after money actually wants to grow, from feeling small to feeling greater by attracting people's attention and respect in his own eyes. Desire is not wrong, neither is the object of desire wrong. You can kill a man with a gun and also save somebody's life with it. So the gun itself is not wrong, it is what you do with it that determines what is wrong. Greed makes desire wrong. We need to honour the world of things, not criticise them. You just need to understand that when you live in a world with ego, you are dead to the live, present moment and instead alive to dead material things. Instead of living the reality you virtually start living in the world of things.

Secret to Fulfilling Desires

If you remove the desire for objects mentally, you will be left with a lot of energy. With this energy you can be creative, spontaneous and produce results by working and not just thinking about what you want. All your goals can be achieved after that. The problem with people is, instead of enjoying the energy, they want to enjoy objects. Why can't we wake up? If we simply look around we find sad faces. These faces cheer up only after one or two drinks go in or when someone appreciates them. Even then, the intoxication disappears the moment something as minor as a tiff with their wives takes place. Money is great but one has to learn the art of earning and spending it.

Life is not about objects but rather about experiencing it and that is entirely subsumed in the race to the top, in collecting money, being better than others and experiencing pleasure instead of bliss (which does not need anything in order to be experienced). People are trading the experience of living with objects. Objects are the by-product of right living and are there to give us physical comforts. When the wants disappear, you realise that you already have what you need, that is, peace and bliss. Once you come to this realisation, creativity flows and your intuition guides you to these rather than running after objects and suffering the consequences. You are home.

How to Know that You are Attached?

If you get disturbed when your expectation is not fulfilled or your opinion is not taken seriously, you are attached to your expectation/opinion.

Absent to Who We Are

We completely forget who we are once we start to identify with the material world. The objects start to look dearer than our own inner peace and calm. Notice how you react when there is a scratch on your car. The person who bangs your car apologises but you are not aware of your consciousness, your being, not aware of whom you have chosen to be at that moment. You are hurt and angry. You suffer. Now the man, who may be on a bike, apologises, but it doesn't make any difference to you. You don't think about what he must be going through. You have car insurance, yet, the hurt gets so overwhelming that it hijacks all your consciousness, your life, values, all that you had thought of yourself. All the decisions and resolutions you had made, to not to get angry and stay calm, all go up in smoke.

Your whole consciousness becomes malefic and you are reduced to nothing but anger. You are no longer a loving, compassionate and forgiving human being, you are your anger. And now since you don't know how to transcend this emotion, all your actions stem from anger. Whatever you do now will be a mere reaction as you are no longer in control, it is hate. You cannot be peaceful if you are not free from the emotional disturbances that the ego is creating.

Irrespective of situations and what people say and do, one should be in sync with his internal energy. All efforts should be put in to attain balance on the inside.

Cause of Disturbance

The ego keeps identifying with whatever it feels will give it a facelift and some importance. You won't let go of things that you are attached to till you realize that what you are attached to are mere stones in comparison to the diamonds available without attachment. Nothing, absolutely nothing has got to do with who you are. The moment you stop deriving your identity from attachments, they disappear on their own. To drop the identity that comes from attachments, avoid measuring yourself through the success you have achieved and don't let the size of your house or car determine your life. Let the deciding factor of your life be consciousness, remain fully awake for each and every moment, don't spend life waiting for that one day or someday.

Remember, trying to drop attachments will create another attachment with non-attachment and will just be another trick of the ego. The secret is to just become conscious of your attachment to things; the ego will vanish on its own. The very awareness of attachments severs the attachment. Consciousness creates a distance between you and the attachment thereby dissolving the impact caused, that is, anxiety and pain.

**Only men are free, have the freedom to use
their mind and not get used by it.**

Consciousness Technique

Doing what is right out of kindness, love and compassion will attract good towards you. Allowing the right to surface rather than trying to change the wrong will free you from the ego. When you do bad karma, you start living in hell. Your ego is your hell. Detachment is knowing that one can build a house but still be homeless from the inside, in spirit. Knowing this will fill you with energy and give you more strength to pursue things joyfully.

5

Developing the Eye to See the 'I'

In order to increase the presence of consciousness and getting rid of the ego, it's very important to be able to recognise the ego in the first place. It is only possible to observe it in action, in the way it makes us feel and act, and identify the conditioned mental processes that self-multiply for further development of the ego. We can see the main aspects of the ego and how they operate in us and reflect onto others through us. When we are able to see the ego working within us, we start becoming conscious, coming closer to our original nature. A lion is ferocious by nature, a cow is calm and a human being is loving, compassionate and intelligent by nature. Our aim is to know and live according to our true self, our consciousness.

The Fearful Ego

Our biggest enemy is fear. Whenever and wherever the ego gets hurt, it converts the perpetrator into its greatest fear. The ego is always insecure because it keeps looking for things that don't exist and is incapable of producing something meaningful from what is there.

Fear is a by-product of your attachment to a thing or even an idea. You love your job and this same love triggers your fears: you might lose the job. The boss may start showing someone else appreciation and god forbid that happens, even though it is bound to, it sets a precedent in your mind. Now this precedent comes to the fore in all other areas of your life as well. You start doubting everything. You take that experience of rejection from the past very personally and which becomes the foundation of fear in you in your mind. Simply put, once bitten twice shy.

Since we are not present, the ego makes us feel false emotions. We might feel that the boss prefers another employee, but this is our interpretation and may not be the reality, it might be a lie that our insecurities lead us to believe. We make it the reality by reacting to the thought and the boss too might respond, seeing our reactive behaviour.

The Moment You Run Away, Fear Takes Over

Instead of dealing with things, you try to escape. Escapism takes your attention away from the situation at hand and diverts it towards making you feel secure psychologically. However, when you face a situation head on, there is no fear at all. When there is no fear, there are greater emotional resources available to produce positive energy. This energy can be used to create whatever you want, rather than hopelessly waiting for your expectations to be fulfilled. It is this very energy that catapults your actions to the next level.

Consciousness Technique: Observing Fear as it Arises

Observe, *fear is the movement of thought.* There is no fear in the now. To access the present moment and be fearless, one has to get rid of the thought which is causing it. How can you think in the present? You can only think about the past, which comes from your memory, or dream about the future, what may happen. Most people end up living in fear as they stick to thoughts that create fear, instead of living in the present and accepting the reality of the situation. They try to run away from the reality.

With fear plaguing it, the mind has to make constant efforts and does not flow like water. Observe the fear-filled thoughts that lead you to continuously imagining consequences. As you become more and more aware of them, your intelligence which was not functioning earlier when you were having inner conflicts, begins to function. Intelligence is overpowered by fearing and foreseeing the future. In the presence of intelligence, fear subsides as intelligence itself presents you with ways to tackle the situation.

Life unfolds when you live from your consciousness, being yourself. And then you don't desire anything from anyone, which dispels the fears.

A mind that makes conscious efforts to defeat fear struggles and remains stuck because of its habit of constant analysing. Whereas when you just observe the working of the mind, it ceases its operations and calms down. The fear disappears. The fear is never because of the situation but because of the thought of the situation.

When your mind is making an effort, you look for results and when just observing, you are not looking for a result. There is a total change that takes place. The mind is available to see things clearly when not seeking.

Is Being Fearless Possible?

Desire itself creates fear as the thought of losing or not getting something comes with it. When I let my future remain free from the burden of shouldering my past and allow life to take its course, there is no fear. Fear comes when we keep waiting for the result of our efforts. We don't believe that when one is moving, he will reach somewhere. When you move ahead according to what you feel is right, you reach your destination. But if you keep falling back on your ego, you miss everything. Life unfolds when you follow your nature; then there is no fear. The only problem is that today people are so disconnected with themselves that they don't know what their true self is, what their consciousness is. So they live in doubt and fear. They are aware of other people's natures and not their own. They will mould themselves according to what others like or don't like. Life unfolds when you live from your consciousness, being yourself. And then you don't desire anything from anyone, which dispels the fears.

Being Yourself – Finding Your Nature

In order to be yourself, you have to possess self-knowledge. Till then all your thoughts will stem from the egoistic mind and you will always be someone else, a pretender.

What if someone is a jerk? Is it okay for him to just be himself? How about people who are scared of being around others and live a hermit-like life, avoiding people? The person who is an idiot to others and the person who is afraid of social situations are both not truly being themselves. Their real self is covered up with conditioned, fear-based thinking. Our true self is who we really are when we let go of all of the stories, labels, and judgments that we have placed upon ourselves. It is who we naturally are without the masks, cover-ups and pretenses. It is who we really are when we let go off what we have taken from other people. There are many people who call themselves social drinkers, who smoke just to look cool and who claim to be themselves by shouting, "This is who I am!", but this is only a façade, it is not who they are. One's true self is completely honest in thought and action, and has the courage to say what one feels without hurting others. Notice many of us lie just to save our skin and look good in other people's eyes. Not finding excuses and not blaming others for your behaviour will help you be yourself.

Courage comes when you are yourself and it gives you the freedom and the ability to be yourself. When you expect something good, you are bound by that expectation. Freedom is when you are free from the bondage of craving and the conflict and sorrow that arise from this bondage. Freedom means to be able to function with what you have and not waiting for the right situations. It frees you from the slavery of situations, circumstances and the events that take place in your life. Waiting only means bondage by what you are waiting for. Independence and freedom arise when you are left alone to deal with things and you deal rather than escape.

Becoming More Aware of Your Thoughts

I used to be shocked by the number of unconscious thoughts that raced through my mind on any given day. My reality began to take shape according to the orders of these conditioned unconscious thinking patterns. Gradually I became more aware of the quality of my thinking. If you allow yourself to sit quietly every morning before starting your day for just five to ten minutes you will find the key. Yes, thoughts will come and go, but just allowing them to do that, without getting attached to them, is magical. Just observe them. When you are finished, continue observing the mind throughout your day. We have so many unconscious beliefs that were probably handed down to us by somebody else, and we believed these to be an integral part of who we are. But becoming more aware of the quality of your thoughts, letting go of the old beliefs, and becoming aware can help in revealing your true nature. We are all so much more than those old negative thinking patterns would ever allow us to believe.

The more you try to run away from something, the more it drives your life.

Are You Living a Predetermined Life?

When you are disempowered, you are living a predetermined life. I recently met an elderly person at a leading corporate house who had a very sour face. We were doing a training program on Stress-free Living. So I was making them realise how they can transcend from expecting love to giving love as expecting causes stress. This elderly gentleman stood up and said, "I have one fear. I have experienced, when I give love, I don't get it back in the same proportions." As if you are given a parameter to measure how much you are getting. I told that man, "Can't you see? Your fears are born from your assumptions". He said, "I know, whatever I do, my wife will remain the same". Since he is operating from the ego, which only knows how to want, he is restricting the flow of his own love. He does not even know what might transpire in his own being if he loves freely and accepts the wife. When you accept anything that is making you uncomfortable, the unease disappears.

The more you try to run away from something, the more it drives your life.

When you assume something, the mind starts to think only around the assumed situation. When one is assuming, the thinking is somewhat like this: *if I help my wife in the kitchen today, then I would have to help her daily. If I work hard today, my boss will give me a tougher assignment next time.* Because of such worries, one is missing the joy today. Can you see the absurdity of it? You are creating your own fears and suffering because of your own contradicting commitments. You want to be successful but want to work less. Fear is the problem that doesn't allow us to see things the way they are. When in fear we don't see "what is" but we see what we are scared of and it becomes a vicious cycle. The ego is not interested in seeing whose fault it is or learning something, it is destructive and wants to destroy any threats to it. Ego perceives threats and then whatever it suggests is violent and fearful.

Whenever you do something out of fear, your mind becomes the ground for more fear to breed. Fear takes away your power to go out into the unknown and try new things.

The Pursuit of Permanent Security Causes Fear

You do not create your life, it is given to you. You have no contribution in it. You don't get to choose your parents. You don't get to choose the way you look. Birth is not in your hands, neither is death. Where is the reason to be anxious? One gets anxious when he tries to control the future, control the outcome of things. But the fact is that this life is given to us and we should be grateful instead of demanding security from an absolutely insecure life. The ego is always on the prowl for greater security and anything which is always searching cannot lead to stability. The ego is always in motion, it has been trained to give you stability in an unstable world. There is no stability. Can anyone guarantee that your heart won't stop beating right now, that your kidneys won't fail, that the currency notes you have saved won't be demonitised or that the ceiling won't fall on you?

I remember once, when I was a child, I was playing carom with my brother and the ceiling fan fell on our heads. Although we were safe, I learnt the lesson of a lifetime. Be prepared for anything and everything. Anything can happen anytime, and that's the design of life. Until and unless you come to terms with this fact, you will remain anxious because the ego will be in a conflict, trying desperately to settle down just as life unsettles you. This divide will create fear. When you are disturbed by fear and anxiety, even a small mosquito looks like an elephant and you feel overpowered by it as the ego tries to conquer everything. Ego is never stable; it is forceful and manipulative. The moment you become present, ego-filled thoughts cease and there are no more thoughts that bother you. You feel calm within and this very calmness is the experience of bliss, joy and happiness.

You can be free of anxieties when you fit in your life so rhythmically, so harmoniously that whatever you do becomes your joy and whatever you get becomes your bliss. When you avoid looking at the outcomes of your actions and stay true to your consciousness, you actually start living. Otherwise, people are waiting to live when their wishes get fulfilled. Presence gives a stable mind from where capabilities and abilities will also start growing.

All events and people are neutral by themselves. It's how we interpret them that makes them what and who they become for us. FEAR is 'False Evidence Appearing Real'. The husband, from before, is unable to live with the wife as his criteria for the ideal wife never got fulfilled. He has seen the films, observed poor relationships and out of that made a sketch of what he perceives to be an ideal wife. Now he has the blueprint of something that doesn't exist and tries to match it with the reality. An assumed map is used to see and change the reality and when it doesn't happen, he gets scared. A weak soul assumes and gets frightened. A soul that understands life on a deeper level, understands that there are many things he can't control and that makes him fearless. We are subject to birth, sickness, aging and death. This is a fact, without awareness of death, life can only be lived on a shallow level. Only after accepting this can we live without fear. When we don't face our fears, we die a little every day because of the crippling effect that is a result of living in constant fear. Ego wants permanence. Understanding that nothing is permanent is the source of freedom from this state of permanent anxiety and fear. If nothing is permanent then there is no need to be anxious. As a matter of fact, then everything you get is simply a bonus and something you should be thankful for.

Facing Fears

One day, in the plains of Africa, a young buffalo named Walter approached his dad and asked him if there was anything that he should be afraid of. "Only lions, my son," his dad responded. "Oh yes, I've heard about lions. If I ever see one, I'll turn and run as fast as I can," said Walter. "No, that's the worst thing you can do," said the large male. "Why? They are scary and will try to kill me." The father buffalo smiled and explained, "Walter, if you run away, the lions will chase you and catch you. And when they do, they will jump on your unprotected back and bring you down." "So what should I do?" asked Walter. "If you ever see a lion, stand your ground to show him that you're not afraid. If he doesn't move away, show him your sharp horns and stomp the ground with your hooves. If that doesn't work, move slowly towards him. If that doesn't work, charge him and hit him with everything you've got!"

"That's crazy. I'll be too scared to do that. What if he attacks me back?" said the startled young buffalo.

"Look around, Walter. What do you see?" Walter looked at the rest of his herd. There were about 200 massive beasts all armed with sharp horns and huge shoulders. "If ever you're afraid, know that we are here. If you panic and run away from your fears, we can't save you, but if you charge towards them, we'll be right behind you." The young buffalo breathed deeply and nodded. "Thanks Dad, I think I understand."

We all have lions in our worlds. There are aspects of life that scare us and make us want to run away, but if we do, they will catch up with us and take over our lives. Our thoughts will be dominated by the very things that we are afraid of and our actions will turn into mere timid and cautious reactions, not allowing us to reach our full potential. Miracles happen when fears are faced without thinking about "what will happen". Initially, the fear may be there, but it is a choice. Choice, because either you get scared and stop or you surpass the thought and move forward with courage and a correct approach. Always choose what you want to do instead of being dejected by your own limiting thoughts that keep telling you why or what you can't do.

Egoistic Anger

It's very important to protect your mind from ego-based anger. But before that, let's see what anger is. Anger can erupt on feeling tired, stressed or irritated. We also feel irritated when our basic human needs like food, shelter, sex, sleep, etc., are not met or are threatened in some way. We also become angry when reacting to other people's frustrations, criticism and warnings and this is not necessarily an inappropriate reaction. Other people's beliefs, opinions and actions too trigger anger in us, affecting our ability to communicate effectively. This makes us more likely to say and do unreasonable or irrational things. Being unreasonable or irrational can lead to others around us feeling threatened, resentful or angry themselves and, again make us react to their reaction. Anger can also be a secondary emotion when feeling sad, frightened, threatened or lonely. It is very important to try to understand why you or somebody else is feeling angry at any given moment so that the root causes can be addressed and problems solved. Anger, however, is not just a state-of-mind but can also have physical manifestations including an increased heart rate, blood pressure and levels of hormones such as adrenaline which prepare us, physically, for the 'fight or flight' response. Due to these physical effects, long-term anger can be detrimental to health and wellbeing. However, here we will take a look at egoistic anger which causes the real damage.

The problem lies with ego-based anger where we keep creating psychological memories that are filled with hurt, hatred, frustration and anxiety. Egoistic anger comes from the beliefs of "being right" and "knowing better" than others. Observe how a majority of the times we want to prove how right we are. Egoistic anger primarily comes into the picture where one has "been" unable to prove his dominance or gets dominated by others, leading to feelings of victimisation. It makes us angry when someone betrays us and carries out perceived injustice towards us.

This is the best source to catch the ego in action as after every reaction that comes from the ego, you regret your reaction.

Spotting Egoistic Anger

Many times the ego takes command, telling you what a "stupid idiot" you are for overreacting; contrarily, the reactions stemming from our consciousness will not be adversarial and will be easy to stop, too. But egoistic anger seems to be unstoppable. Anger arising from consciousness will not make you feel bad. So spotting ego-based anger is very easy; it makes you feel bad after expressing. You will feel as if something came over you, possessed you and when you yelled, you will feel as if it wasn't you.

I started spotting my ego through anger very easily only after it made my life hell. One of the most deceptive aspects of the ego is that it generates powerful emotional reactions, and then blames us for how it made us feel. I would shout at my mother and convince myself that it was the right thing to do. But no sooner, a process would start inside that made me feel guilty and wonder, *why did I shout, after all she is my mother.* This became a pattern. I would say nasty things to my friends, siblings, colleagues and then repent having done it.

Immediately after an angry outpour, the ego starts an emotional analysis, turning it into a process of inflicting self-criticism and blame. The ego controls introspection which is where you try to reflect. You can become present of the egoistic emotional dramas, as the ego keeps justifying and reaffirming itself and hides behind self-criticism.

You may feel "worthless" because of the critic inside of you, continuously working to pull you down. This is a painful emotion to live with, and in order to mask the pain, you might cover it up with an image of bravado, projecting an image of security and confidence, all the while struggling with feelings of insecurity, worthlessness and inadequacy inside. Confidence that does not come from the ego is markedly different. In this confidence, you don't let things get to your head with your abilities, skills and self-acceptance. Therefore it does not impact your interactions with others. Sometimes humility may also be mistaken for shyness and insecurity. A truly humble person is fully aware and at peace with himself and his surroundings. Confidence without arrogance and humility without insecurity are the cornerstones of consciousness.

I once had a fight with one of my friends on a WhatsApp group. It was my egoistic anger that was making me react to petty things; my emotional block of not being accepted from my childhood got triggered. I got so angry that I left the group. When I tried talking to my friends later at a party, everybody was cold as a cucumber. They reacted by not reacting. According to me, it wasn't a positive response and I felt uncomfortable as I was not heard. Another block was hence added to my existing block of rejection. I was piling up such instances and simultaneously realising that it is impacting my consciousness.

I tried talking to my friends but it didn't work. I tried meditating but, on the contrary, more thoughts of rejection started coming, the only difference was, people were changing; sometimes parents, sometimes friends, sometimes customers, but my fear of being rejected remained constant. It was like a vicious circle; the more I tried getting out of it, the deeper I sank.

I realised that I was carrying anger which made me feel repressed which led to destructive behaviour. I realised that there was no harmony in my energies. When I could forget my anxieties, I would crack jokes and be very lively. Somewhere I started learning that the ego was getting into a groove like neural pathways in the brain after repeating any action or behaviour frequently. Initially, I avoided my friends, but something inside told me that I cannot avoid everyone. These incidents were happening every other day. I didn't want to live like an island, by cutting, destroying, repressing and rejecting anything that life was bringing to me.

I started acting differently from what I was feeling. When I left the group, barring one, no one spoke to me or tried taking me back into the WhatsApp group. Of course, we were meeting in person, but internally I was uneasy. This uneasiness opened lot many things for me to see.

I was crystal clear now that when someone neglects me, and I feel bad about it, instead of working on the feeling I start neglecting that person. I understood that this can never solve anything and once you make it a habit, you keep distancing yourself from people while you should have worked on your inner weakness.

The twist is, my ego was playing games. When that one friend spoke to me, he told me that all other friends want to talk to me but I was in such a rage, that I refused. And the ego very conveniently ignored that bit of information and launched the allegations. I knew that my friends wanted to speak to me but the ego loves drama and the spotlight and does not let you listen to the voice of reason and steals your attention.

When you don't know who you are, you start correcting who others are.

Now we don't have Buddhas all around us who will understand all this and come to you. We need to realise that it was our rage that shut them out in the first place. This very understanding takes you out of the clutter as knowing the truth is the beginning of strength.

Just when I was going through this, the exact same thing happened in another WhatsApp group where one of my friends, Parakram, left the group. He did not have any fight but since we made the group for a reunion after 25 years, he just left for reasons unknown but I understood that he must have left feeling uncomfortable and a loss of connect.

I immediately added him to the group. The moment I did that, I felt as if tons of weight had been lifted off me. But this was still the result of the egoistic games that we need to understand. The ego tries to act like a saint and show that, "See my humility, instead of trying to get even with people; I see other people's pain in such situations".

Had this action come from consciousness, it would not have felt like a burden being shrugged off as there are no burdens when you are present, aware and fully rooted in your consciousness. You feel burdened as the ego starts to derive meaning out of everything. When I started becoming stronger with the growth of my consciousness, I could clearly see that the ego wanted to feel important by either going against the flow or making others go as per its dictates.

Such incidents occur almost daily in people's life in some way or the other. If it is not in the WhatsApp group then it's in the office or at home within the family. It is called a crisis of identity. When you don't know who you are, you start correcting who others are. It's very important to get out of this as it drives you insane.

On the contrary, one should be on the look-out for such situations as they are the stepping stones to transformation. People who are entrenched in such situations and think they know what is right and what is wrong, never blossom. They will continue to live a dull, routine and boring life and are crippled by the effect of their egos that makes them struggle every day to win.

Similar situations will arise even when you are in your consciousness, it's just that there won't be any good or bad attributed to them.

The moment you are present and start seeing the mechanism behind all the good and bad, when you start seeing that they are all socially manufactured things that your ego produces, you will get in touch with your consciousness. Those who seek transformation should know this. All such situations are neutral and there is no good or bad but because of your reactive mind they become events to remember and make you suffer. If you choose mentally from right or wrong, you stay divided and split from within. In such situations if you avoid choosing who is right and who is wrong, you will remain sound otherwise this choice won't let you relax and you will keep justifying your stand and condemn others.

When you are dealing with people, you have to keep in mind that they too are conditioned the way you are. For them, good and bad exists. It's imperative to be courteous to them and their views. It is not for you to disturb anybody's beliefs. It is stupid to interfere as you will be interfering with your own peace of mind.

Our societies are designed in a way that doesn't let us be honest and express what we truly feel, the outcome is not realising that being yourself is the only happiness that's there. Knowing this, we should express ourselves, just being careful that throughout our expression we don't hurt anybody. Our expression should not become the cause of someone else's emotional blocks.

When you grapple with life's situations and people in a neutral way, your consciousness remains whole and centred. You become a wizard and convert your ego to consciousness. It's always your decision, whether to participate or avoid the mental ego games. Remember it's a role that you need to play. There is nothing in the situations, things and people outside but whatever is, is in the inner depths of your consciousness. When you go with the flow of life, knowing that you have to just play a role and not get attached to what it throws at you, you start sailing. This is true strength.

When our strengths increase, troublesome situations start getting weaker.

Ego: A Meaning-Making Machine

The ego reduces reality to its own limited understanding. Any words spoken to a man who is being operated by his ego do not make any difference. His ego interprets the meaning according to its own understanding and mental state when the word is spoken, instead of seeing the intention of the person who is speaking. That's why we see many obstinate people who are more interested in having their point of views understood than understanding themselves. Whatever we see and experience, we give it a name and label it on the basis of what we already know. We rarely see anything new beyond the screen of these recorded words, making us dead to the present and alive to the dead past. So when we label something we are unable to feel that something as our consciousness is asleep. Basing our interpretation on the meaning of the word with which the mind is associating it, we react.

A dog barks on the street, it's early morning and you are going to the office. Hearing the dog's bark your meaning-making machine remembers the dog that your neighbour, Pinky, had 20 years ago. You start thinking about Pinky. What a beautiful girl she was. You remember how you used to stare at her when she came back from school. You remember her cute smile and the way she used to return your smile. Now you start thinking that it would have been so great had you married her and not your present wife, Shashikala. Now you start thinking how bad Shashikala is and how good Pinky would have been, if only you had a job at that time and her father had not refused your proposal. Life could have been so good and different only if Pinky was in your life. But you don't know that Pinky's husband is also thinking the same thing when his neighbour's dog barks.

Your Word is Your World

Once, while working, one of my friends, who was assisting me, asked me to pass her the purse that was kept on a table near me. I turned towards the table but couldn't see it. She asked again, and I said, "There is no purse." She turned around from her side and picked up the purse. Now I couldn't see it because the moment she said "purse", the image that formed in my mind was that of a men's wallet, because in my mind, the word 'purse' stood for a pocket-sized flat folding case for holding money and plastic cards, mostly used by men. I couldn't see what was lying right in front of me because I was looking for something else. I stuck to my mental image of the word "purse" and not the actual purse lying on the table. We similarly often miss what is right in front of us.

Words are like a screen before our eyes and one speck of dust can obstruct the humongous Himalayas in front of us.

Notice we are mere puppets in the hands of words. Words are the ego's centre, from where it operates. The moment you say 'boss' or 'wife', your ego comes up with a whole array of words, positive or negative. Keep noticing, all the words that are installed in your ego are a world by themselves. Your word is creating your world, whether at the level of the thought or in the way they are spoken. The way you see yourself is through words and people also see us through words and we see them through words, too. The problem is when we speak to others, they are interpreting our words as per their understanding of the word and not the way we are saying it. These little words form the labels that we attach to people and things around us.

Imagine, your boss is scolding you for your bad performance and all you keep asking yourself is, "Who made him the boss? Is he good or bad? What's his problem? Is this right or wrong, what's the answer? Is this true or false? What's the solution? Should I agree or disagree? What's in it for me or for him? Should I trust or mistrust? Should or shouldn't I? Because of his scolding, I have no peace. Why me? How? When? Where?" It's like you are hit by a bullet, you're bleeding profusely and your ego goes on asking, "Who shot the bullet, what is the person's name, where does he belong? Was the bullet from a .22 pistol, was it made out of brass or iron?" You are hit and are bleeding profusely. What should be your first priority, finding the details your ego asks for or going to the doctor to get treated? You lose your job. What does this mean? It means nothing; it is a fact that you have lost your job and that's all there is to it. The ego tries to ascribe meaning to everything. It will terrorise you, "Now what will happen, how I will survive, how I will pay the bills" and so on and so forth.

This excessive analysis of words makes you resigned and cynical. Even before doing something, egoistic fear makes you think so much that the action doesn't happen as over-analysing can get paralyzing. The first priority should be to secure a job. Then there will be no fear as you are acting on what should be acted upon instead of reacting to what happened. Many people are unsuccessful, not because they can't think, but because they can't stop thinking. This continuous movement of thought creates fear. Ego stops you from acting as it tries to exert control all the time, causing energy to drain. It has made us all control freaks. Dropping your ego helps you get out of the illusion of controlling things.

Egoistic language that stops you:

- *"I know he won't come."* So you don't call and check, rather you just take a decision based on your assumption and don't invite him, needless to say, he doesn't come.

- *"He won't have the money."* So you don't even ask, subsequently your thought wins and you don't get the money.

- *"He won't understand."* So you don't even try explaining it and mentally label him as dumb.

- *"If I don't win, he will blame me. It's better I sit in the stands and laugh at others than play and get blamed and give people a chance to laugh at me."* You don't take the risk of losing and let your ego win.

Being Extraordinary

If you honestly trust your thoughts, which are in words, it is not possible to be extraordinary as they will always pull you down because they operate from the past. But if you see Gandhi – an ordinary man who became extraordinary because he had an extraordinary possibility in language; "I will free India with non-violence." There is no truth there but when you talk powerfully, it's a strong place to be. Your acknowledgement gives rise to a new possibility as the old disempowering possibility was also in language, "I cannot do."

When you get stuck in words, there is no possibility left for you to create something. You go for an interview and think, "I know I won't get through." Now you're restrained by these conversations. We are not equipped to predict the future but that's what the ego keeps doing. Anything coming out of fear will only be a modified form of insecurity. Even if you find a new job in this fearful state, you will fear losing it. This way we make the words that we think come true by following them instead of proving them false. We always have an option of going beyond them by trying to find out the reasons behind what we perceive.

Possibilities Beyond Words

When one is hypnotised by words, he is unable to know the unknowable. When we look at things without labelling them, the reality emerges as the judgmental mind is shut and we start to see things clearly. Since ancient times, mankind has looked up to see birds flying and dreamt of having wings. The Wright brothers were no different. But they could see what others couldn't as they didn't see mere words and envisioned something greater. They made the first plane and today the world is widely connected physically because of them. So when you use thoughts instead of getting used by them, you are able to see the reality and a whole world of possibilities opens up. Language is a mere medium for creation, we shouldn't limit our avenues to the words we use to label things. So when you say, "I am a failure, I failed this." You become a product of that language and all your energy flows into supporting that thought, and then they stop being mere words.

Power of Taking a Stand

When you take a stand and make a declaration saying, "Now I will make it happen", a new energy starts flowing within you, making you competent. The situation is always neutral, but the thought of it looming makes us fear it. Instead of thinking such thoughts, you should use the same energy to pump in positivity and power. Following the same, I am starting to come to terms with my nephew's accident that almost got him killed. The doctors said that his chances of survival were almost zero. When I spoke to my uncle, he made me realise what taking a stand is. He told me, "Shashank, everything is fine and Abhimanyu is a fighter. Nothing will happen to him." And truly, he valiantly fought death, surviving as the walking example of this lesson.

Keeping Integrity Alive for Success

When I repay what is due I feel powerful. Integrity is often thought of as moral uprightness and steadfastness – making the "good" choices, doing the "right thing." In fact, it is far more than that.

It is a home, an anchor, a created and continuing commitment, a way of being and acting that shapes who you are. Integrity is not constrained by, nor does it reside in rules, prescriptions, or imposed demands. It resides in the ability to carry out your word, being true to your principles, and ultimately, being true to yourself. You will discover that integrity results in a life lived as your own person, a life expressing freedom, power and joy.

People become miserable when they break their promises because then they break the trust and faith they have put in themselves. By breaking commitments you might gain some material advantage but you will lose the other person. The tough side of integrity is, you will definitely fail in maintaining it all the time as its very nature is too elusive. That is, it will be violated sometimes due to situations and people. However, such violations have consequences. So the moment you realise that your actions either are not in sync with or defile your integrity, change them to restore it. For example, if you are doing something and you know it to be wrong, don't do it, irrespective of whether or not someone will come to know. Anything you do will have consequences. Life is simple; it works on cause and effect. Whatever you are doing today, is what you will get tomorrow. You should have no qualms about it. See what you are doing today is the result of what you thought yesterday or the efforts you made before. Experience whatever comes your way. Do what you want to do. Keep trying. But don't forget what you already have. Enjoy your parents, your family, children, friends, job, this beautiful body you have, the house you live in, the car you drive and whatever you have been blessed with. If you are working under compulsion, your mind will not function at its best and may not allow you to work with perfection and speed.

If you love yourself, you would not do shoddy, careless and imperfect work. You will know that who you are is how you do things. Your very way of doing things defines you. Then work is a statement of your deepest core. The mind also supports you when you take conscious actions. When you are aware, the mind is not there to distract you; as a matter of fact, it is there for your help. It starts working efficiently as it is centred and does not run haphazardly on the dictates of the blind senses. When you do something, being aware of your potential and not for the salary, you receive appreciation. Your integrity gets demonstrated and your demeanour has a very different glow.

Dependence on anything leads to misery, but so does being independent in the specific context of work. The right thing is to be interdependent while dealing with people and at work. The company needs you as much as you need the company. Then there is equilibrium. The only way to set the balance is to first be perfect in your performance, consistently, irrespective of what you get. Even if your work is initially not recognised by your company, you shouldn't stoop down by reacting negatively. But if you operate from the ego, the only thing that you will do is react and fight with your boss and sow the seed of future failures.

Think about the seeds you have already sown in terms of words, thoughts, attitude and intentions. You will get what you have been giving.

Your work should produce so much energy that there shouldn't be any need to derive it from somewhere else. People choose work on the basis of interests, liking, viability and workability. In fact, one needs to have the right energy to work. This energy can be generated only if a person works with a purpose, of not just earning money but the purpose of contributing to others, the society, to his own life and to live a great life. You don't need to take extra time for yourself, family, and friends if you are producing energy at work. People want to run away from what they do daily by waiting for the weekend or going on a vacation. Fear is the only enemy and when you work without focusing on the outcome, which is called *nishkama karma*, you experience freedom in performing.

When you work and keep thinking of money, you lose focus and the quality of work goes down.

Being present, being available to whatever you do is bliss. When you let your actions operate from the thoughts, you are simply reacting to the dictates of your mind. When happy circumstances come, you get happy, when challenging ones come, you get sad. Who is the person who gets happy and sad? That is your mind and not you. When you discover yourself and your consciousness, you will know who you are beyond your ego and the identities that you have collected. You will then even fall in love with your failures. The beauty of discouragement is, it discourages the mind, but when present, it teaches one to be courageous irrespective of what others say or whatever happens.

You are not your ego, thoughts or feelings but your consciousness that witnesses everything, the seat of bliss, insights, intuitions, creativity and spontaneity. When working with the ego, whatever work you do is a pain. The programming of the mind is such that it sees work as a burden and the ego keeps questioning: *There are people who have not done anything and are still successful, so why am I the only one who has to suffer?*

Transforming the Translations

"I am shy. I am not confident. I am inferior." You are forcefully defining yourself. You have ways of being which you think you are. You pretend to be who you think you are. You alter who you are being by altering the words and you can alter who you are also for others.

Whenever you get discouraged by your thoughts, remember they are nothing without your belief in them. The mind eavesdrops on these words and creates feelings accordingly. Howsoever grave a situation may be, using powerful words will help transform our feelings. Transforming the translation actually amounts to being aware as you are showing the mind who is in control, by not using the harsh words the ego suggests; it may be an abuse or a belittling thought filled with guilt – but with attention changing them. When you do anything that defies the ego's suggestions, you are aware, present and in your consciousness. Slowly and slowly you gain control over the ego. A time will come when you will use your mind the way you use your hands or any other organ or body part. Helen Keller, a blind and deaf student, began reading and a whole new world opened up for her. Language makes you who you are. It's only because of language that you have different ways of being. That's why we don't say 'dog being' or 'cat being' but we say 'human being'. 'Being' is a state of existence, like being happy, being sad, being joyous, etc.

"He doesn't like me", "I hate him", "I will show him" – all these can be translated to, "I will find in me what triggers others or if there is nothing, then there is no need to worry, others have to figure it out." "I am present to the hate within me; I will pause and look what instigated that energy by looking at my beliefs". "I will drop the 'I' that needs to get even with people and simply love them".

Transforming the translation of old words puts the past back where it belongs. For creation you need reality, that is the present moment. There is no world out there. The words you use are creating your world.

Sachin Tendulkar was once invited by a baseball team to play a match when he was in the US. The next morning, he went there and was asked to bat. The pitcher was seven feet tall. Tendulkar's mind started chattering, thinking, *oh my God, how I will face this man. I have never played baseball in my whole life.* He got scared and got out. He then told the pitcher, "Just give me a minute."

He went to the corner and talked to himself. He transformed the translation of the words that his mind was doing unconsciously.

He said to himself, *firstly, I am Sachin Tendulkar, I have faced Shoaib Akhtar, the fastest bowler, why am I getting scared? This man is nothing in front of me. Secondly, full toss is the easiest ball to play in cricket.* He came back and struck a big hit. The baller got surprised, as he had sensed nervousness on Tendulkar's face earlier. He asked, "What did you do?" Tendulkar said, "Nothing, just changed the translation of a few words." What Sachin Tendulkar did was just change how the ball appeared to him. Your self-knowledge becomes "distinctive" and shapes the way you see the way the world occurs to you. A distinction is from where you see, like a window to ponder upon. It is how things appear to you in your understanding. For example, your mother appears to you the way she does because of the experiences of the past. She does not appear as a mother to someone else. So mother is a "distinction". The moment you hear the word "mother", a whole world opens up for you. There is no person, no situation out there in the world. They only appear the way they do to you because of your distinctions. When you get threatened, you see the other person or the situation through words and not what you can do with them or it. When you keep altering the appearance, from "I am this" to "this is who I am", your ego keeps getting transformed.

No New Action = No New Result = No New Future = No Transformation

When you don't cover up things, people and situations with words and avoid labelling them, new possibilities open up. Instead of getting possessed by thoughts and the spell of words, you start using them to transform your old ways of looking at things. You start feeling new. Ego, with its words, reduces reality. The problem lies with labelling others and forming images for yourself.

Labelling leads to limitations and limitations arise because of labelling.

You can stop resorting to egoistic language whenever you want to. Just be present to the moment and act with the present moment's awareness. Simply avoid getting sucked into the stories the ego tells you. It's just about communicating in the right way that is appropriate as per the situation with yourself and others that makes wonders.

Being a Powerful Communicator

Communication is a word derived from communion and the word communion from union, which means oneness. When you communicate, you are one with the other person. There is no barrier of egos. With consciousness, you develop the ability to see through words. Words are mere containers. The meaning of your communication lies in the response you get. To understand this, one needs to develop pristine listening because the skill of speaking depends on listening. What you hear, the meaning you take out is what you respond to. It's intelligent to avoid complaining and being a victim, you should instead be tactful in your communications. What you say is not as important as the way you say it. Most people listen to not your words but the accompanying tone and emotions. Expressing in a way that doesn't hurt others and also makes you feel relaxed and unburdened helps you become present. This can happen when you don't speak out of fear. Considering the consequences of whatever you do helps and it keeps increasing your consciousness. When you speak or do something, you are not present, you become what you speak and do. Then you don't communicate with people, you actually communicate with yourself.

6

Puppets in the Hands of the Ego

Comfort Zones

The ego derives comfort and security from past experiences. Sticking to your comfort zone means living in a world of the past, to experience that which is already experienced. When we are controlled by our ego, we don't want to risk the unknown and put aside our beliefs. We don't even want to listen to the other person's point of view. Blaming others is the easiest thing to do. The ego always tries to avoid things which are beyond its comprehension and not in accordance with its expectations which it builds on the basis of memories. Therefore, we are always operating at a sub-optimal level; our capacities are limited by the ego and are not enabled by conscious resolve. Notice when you want to do something, you have the capacity. But when your confidence waivers and you wonder whether or not you will be able to do it, it is a thought coming from the ego which judges and evaluates itself on the basis of past experiences and tells you – "You can't do this, forget it." The ego lives in the past and therefore does not live on real facts, which are being established in the present; it does not make its own resolves and a majority of its actions come from what it is conditioned into, what others have said, what its beliefs are. The ego gets limited as its "I can" and "I cannot" are fixed and remain static even in a dynamic world. Getting out of your comfort zone is doing things beyond your limited self.

When you don't understand how things work from your own experiences, you will depend on external situations and people to run your life. This pattern of expecting from others and situations is definitely comfortable but your behaviour and thought processes will also become dependent and then you will react like a machine to whatever stimulus or situations you face, looking all the while, for a challenge-free life. This comfortable way of living has made us tremendously uncomfortable and now we are comfortable with the uncomfortable things as well.

There are people who get used to their boss's scolding; their wife's nagging, living in a smelly place and their mind's constant chatter too. They reach a stage where they get used to both, internal and external disturbances. If one gets used to disturbances and does not take any action to remove them, it is an indication that the mind has become totally dull. It becomes so because you avoid facing the truth; you are not aware of your own reactions and the various agitated states of your being. You get used to the external as well as the internal commotion.

A mind occupied with unpleasant past moments has no future and will be an erratic, dull mind.

Why Laziness

When you are operating out of consciousness, your actions are spontaneous, as there is energy. All laziness, therefore, is a result of lack of energy and nothing else. You are not lazy because you don't feel like doing a particular thing, you are lazy because you don't have the energy to do things. Your energy is sapped by the ego's perpetually flawed interpretations of the present through a prism of memories and judgment from the past. The focus of creative energy is instead on either bothering or hurrying.

Heights of ignorance and cynicism are achieved when you get so lazy that you stop noticing the pain you are living in. Till the time you see the pain, the sorrow, the sadness that's there in your life, you won't act and work on your egoistic mind to set it right.

I see people drinking alcohol daily and then going to the temple and chanting mantras to attain peace. They are blind to the pain that they are living in. They keep blaming their husbands, wives, bosses and life in general for the condition that they are in. Not realizing that they are in this condition as a result of their blindness to their egoistic mind, which has made them too comfortable. Instead of taking some action to work on it, they keep living in a false world, hoping that someday, when they have respect, a big house or a big car, everything will settle in place.

The only thing people living in comfort zones do, whether they have money or not, is worry.

Comfort Zone is Your Enemy

The other day I read a beautiful article on the net by Team Fearless on beating the comfort zone. The gist of the article was that one of the biggest ironies of life is that the harder you try to stay comfortable, the more life makes you uncomfortable. It's true, life will throw more and more problems your way. Life will keep flinging rocks at you, it will keep resisting you, keep creating struggles and issues.

And because people are so concerned about being comfortable instead of concerning themselves with growing, they keep struggling, because they don't want to address their limitations and move beyond them. Life is the way it is. There is something wrong with being comfortable and yet, whatever comes your way, you blame it for being the source of your discomfort.

Many people have bank balances but nothing else, and the worst part is, they don't even know what else there is to have.

You are here to grow. And if you don't make yourself uncomfortable, life itself will push you out of your comfort zone. So you have two options. Either you commit to constant growth and feeling of discomfort on your own accord and become the master of your destiny, or you hand over the reins and let life happen to you by default. One path leads you to success and the other path leads to constant struggle and pain. It's your choice.

Don't waste time forwarding WhatsApp messages or playing mobile games and procrastinating. Why do you run the moment your friend texts you to come and have a few drinks? You have got to be willing to make hard decisions. You've got to be willing to feel uncomfortable, to feel awkward, to face rejection, to fail, to feel pressure. You've got to be willing to face those things, because that is what is necessary for you to grow out of your egoistic mind.

How many times have you looked back at your life and said, "Man, if I only knew then what I know now, I would have lived my life so differently."

The only way for you to develop knowledge and awareness is to try things you have not yet tried. To do things you have not yet done, to create things you have not yet created, to go to places you have not yet explored. That is how you grow!

That is how you become the person who is worthy of lounging with their favourite drink; life rewards you with those experiences AFTER you do the work.

Start making those calls, start approaching that person, start practicing kindness and compassion, ignore the feelings of jealousy and greed, confront your anxiety, hit the gym, study harder, begin waking up early even if you're not a morning person, put an end to procrastination. Start doing the things that you know within your heart you should have started doing a long time ago so that you can build the experiences and the knowledge that you need to succeed. Don't read this as some sermon. Read this as a direct sign, a direct message that life is giving you, to wake you up, to help you acknowledge your own greatness, your own consciousness.

When you push yourself into discomfort, your friends will take notice, your colleagues will take notice, your family will take notice, LIFE will take notice, and life will begin to back you up. Life will begin to support you and open doors for you and introduce you to the people who will take you to the next level, but you have got to take the first step! So take it.

Once there was a king who received a gift of two magnificent falcons. They were peregrine falcons, the most beautiful birds he had ever seen. He gave the precious birds to his head falconer to be trained. Months passed and one day the head falconer informed the king that though one of the falcons was flying majestically, soaring high in the sky, the other bird had not moved from its branch since the day it had arrived. The king summoned healers and sorcerers from all over to tend to the falcon, but no one could make it fly. He presented the task to the members of his court, but the next day, the king was told that the bird had still not moved from its perch.

Having tried everything else, the king thought to himself: *Maybe I need someone more familiar with the countryside to understand the nature of this problem.* So he cried out to his court, "Go and get a farmer." In the morning, the king was thrilled to see the falcon soaring high above the palace gardens. He said to his court, "Bring me the doer of this miracle." The court quickly located the farmer who came and stood before the king. The king asked him, "How did you make the falcon fly?" With his head bowed, the farmer said to the king, "It was very easy, your highness. I simply cut the branch the bird was sitting on."

Follow Your Intuition

We fail to follow our intuition when we listen to the ego and always oblige others. Many people stick to unfulfilling jobs because they are so afraid of what other people would think of them for failing that they don't dare step out of their comfort zones.

I started noticing my ego getting caught up in the stories and labels in my head as I started becoming comfortable with a mediocre life. I woke up when I caught myself playing roles with others in my thoughts. It was like a secret movie playing all the time. When I was able to catch myself, I felt pathetic because I cared so much about being accepted by others that I nearly lost track of who I was. When it got too much, I asked myself, *if I don't care about what others think of me, what would my actions be?* With this one statement, I realized that who I naturally am is perfectly okay and I don't need anything else to complete myself. The moment you align yourself with joy and calm, when you let go of the old ways of thinking, start following your bliss, and doing what you love, you are out of the comfort zone. You connect to your true nature through your intuition and you start getting out of the clutches of the ego.

Magic happens when we follow those tiny urges. When we keep following our intuition even in the midst of the rough roads, we are guided towards our purpose of life. For me, it started when I followed my intuition and it made me quit one of my last assignments in a training company itself where I was failing, which was actually the way out, a way to be my true self. Sometimes failing leads us to the right thing that our soul urges to do. I had no clue what I would do, but my intuition kept guiding me. I landed back on my feet with my own training company. Earlier also I was training but as an employee. In your case, you don't need to leave your job but can start with small tasks like making a phone call, replying to emails or choosing a different way of working. When you do this with small things, courage for the big things will automatically start building up. Aligning yourself with your true nature is the most important thing. Inside your comfort zone you will always remain shy, isolated, depressed and irritated but never yourself. It is important to love and accept yourself wherever you are at the moment, maybe in a relationship or work but with consciousness and not without awareness.

The Way Out of Comfort Zones

- Develop a tendency of remaining present in your mind.

- See your comfort zone as a cage. Choose constructive discomfort. Avoid taking the safe, comfortable and known path. Choose courage over being comfortable. Set goals that force you to get out of your comfort zone. Practice being uncomfortable.

- Don't dash out of your comfort zone, take tiny but regular steps.

- Check your progress from time to time.

- Do something, almost anything differently to see what happens.

- Shift the attention from thoughts of blame and hurt to the present moment.

- Just listen without judging and you will notice new opportunities coming up.

- Take some time out and have a good look at yourself and your fears.

Don't focus on what you want to become but focus on what you want to do.

Don't wait for the right time or the right things; just do the right things on time.

People who wait for certain conditions never accomplish anything. Set your own terms through your work, intention, attention and action. Keep the faith – if you have faith the size of a mustard seed you can move mountains. Results depend on many factors. What we have in our hands is just doing our best, that's why action is important. Thinking doesn't get you any new ideas or anywhere in life. It simply operates from the known, the past. The past has already given you what it had to give you. To get something new, you need to be in action. When you are in action, great and novel things come out of it. Live life with what you have. That's the charm and the challenge. If life has given you a lemon, make lemonade out of it, for God's sake! Make something out of it.

Stop whining about how you feel, what you should have got, could have got… Live in the reality and not in a make-believe world. What you want and what you should have got are expectations that you have built up. Reality is what you have right now, your possessions, your people, your skill sets, your experiences, your thoughts and your intentions. Just be aware of the opportunities around you when you feel you are struggling. Whenever life has made me struggle, it has also given me a new direction, matching my nature. Life at times forces us in directions that we ought to have found for ourselves. Just don't listen to those voices in your head telling you that you can't do this. Don't let anybody tell you that you can't do something. Not even yourself. Don't accept weak thoughts from yourself as well. You have got to dream and protect that dream. People who can't do something themselves, they tell you that you can't do it either. You want something, just go get it. Period! Just take chances without any fear and play the game. Be driven by inspiration and not desire, working intuitively. Inspiration is a divine influence on your soul that is not dependent on outcomes. Always remember, your success in comparison to others does not define who you are, what defines you is how well you get up after every fall.

The fun is in your self-expression, expressing something that you believe in deep down your heart, not in craving for success and respect from people who themselves don't have self-respect and are massive failures themselves as far as living joyfully is concerned. Many people have bank balances but nothing else, and the worst part is, they don't even know what else there is to have. They are completely oblivious to inner beauty. Just make your life your way and not the way people want. Get out of the habit of living for others, now! Just don't fight, stay humble but also keep doing your own thing. Learn from your mistakes quickly and make your next move. When you deal with something on your own, it gives you power. The very expectation of support is weakness. The person who needs support cannot be a support to anyone else. Commitments of the mind might fail but those that rise from knowingness that comes from being present can't fail because consciousness itself is the way. Working with awareness

When you deal with something on your own, it gives you power. The very expectation of support is weakness.

will also ensure the quality of your work, not because the boss will appreciate it but because you will feel the need to do everything in the right and perfect way. And this way your actions will inspire others to dream more, learn more and do more, making you their leader.

To get to consciousness and out of the ego's habitual ways, never criticise your company, boss or anyone else for that matter. Negative talk only destroys us and makes us frustrated. Use the negative talk to know that you need to focus on handling the situation. This will help transform the electro-dynamic field, the aura that surrounds you. This new powerful aura won't let you do wrong as it will enhance the presence in you. It will bring you back the moment you go back to the past or do something counterproductive. To do something wrong, you need a very different kind of aura. Work as per situations and not as per your preconceived attitudes. If the situation demands that you do extra work, do it. Adaptability is the biggest skill as it comes from consciousness. People driven by the mind become rigid as the mind wants only what it already knows. People who are self-motivated don't work for money, they work for self-contentment. the outcome becomes secondary to them as their work itself charges them. If you are present even for a minute while working, you will

> *To do something wrong, you need a very different kind of aura. Work as per situations and not as per your preconceived attitudes.*

realise this. It's those times when you get the "flow". The flow refers to a mental state of energized attention and focus, which comes from engagement in tasks that match one's abilities. Tasks that are below our abilities cause boredom, and tasks that are above our abilities cause anxiety. Tasks that match one's abilities are what lead to the flow. To be satisfied and to find the ability to do what one wants, you have to find the flow.

Being In Action

Chanting *Crocin, Crocin, Crocin* continuously will not cure your headache but taking one will. Similarly, reciting someone else's success mantras won't help you succeed. When we operate with consciousness, the inner centre, actions don't spring from conditioned reactions based on fear but from the present moment of awareness. If a snake is inside your room, you won't think about what you should do, you will just do what needs to be done. But upon losing a job, instead of searching for a job, you keep thinking about why this happened to you, you try to convince yourself that it wasn't your fault and so on. When you get centred inside and take charge of your ego, you will have the focus to do everything, especially for worldly achievements. Success is achieved when you give 100 per cent in your efforts for understanding, processing and putting what you learnt to action. This makes you centred from the inside and it brings a sense of responsiveness and intelligence as it comes from a relaxed state of being. Relax now because the ego, the source of all our tension, unease, unhappiness, suffering, reactiveness and anger is not there. The ego ceases to exist when you, the master, are awake.

Knowing others is intelligence; knowing yourself is true wisdom. Mastering others is strength; mastering yourself is true power.

Consciousness Techniques

When you are stuck in the ego's comfortable but vicious energy, live in the present, connect with people, nature, and the environment. Go to the garden and see the green leaves and flowers. Watch birds and animals. Instead of thinking, use your senses to connect with your surroundings.

You can only experience consciousness in waking up from the ashes when you are tired and dead. It's GOOD if a 6.5 feet tall guy plays good basketball but it's GREAT if a 5 feet guy plays well. It's not that significant if you have the wherewithal and then succeed as when you succeed despite not having the means.

Ego Honours the Voice in the Head

Become aware of the way your conditioned mind works by seeing whom is your ego honouring in any given situation. 'Honouring' here means reacting to the voices in your head as if they were commandments. Sometimes we start living according to what we are told and simply follow what we hear; sometimes it is what the astrologer says and sometimes even the weekly newspaper's horoscope.

A man once saw a film where the protagonist, a businessman, had four children. They all grow up very well but his business collapses after he has a fight with his brothers. After watching the film, this 'suggestion' that the businessman failed because he had four children entered this man's mind as he too had four children and was a businessman. And the exact thing happened to him, his business collapsed after having a fight with his brothers, all because of something he picked up from a movie, saw it with emotions, believed in it and by default it got recreated in his life.

An astrologer told one of my friends that his next seven-and-a-half years would be full of struggle. My friend was a hard-working guy, but when he struggled in establishing his new business, the astrologer's voice echoed, "Your next seven-and-a-half years will be rife with struggle". He dropped all efforts of facing the challenge, as now his mind, which was programmed by the astrologer, was controlling his actions. He left the business and took up a job for the next seven years.

Sometimes good suggestions too work wonders. My father's motivating words helped me survive the toughest phase of my life. He told me, "Just keep doing what your heart says and never forget people will be against many things you do, it is much better than you being against yourself."

Ask yourself, whom are you honouring?

The Ego is Blind to the Real World

We miss living life when we live with a certain mindset towards it. All mindsets spring from the ego. Mindsets are artificially created whereas life is not our design and is not created by us. Your attitudes and philosophies act as limitations in experiencing life. When we live with a conditioned mind we try to fit life in the mindset instead of fitting with life.

There is an old story about a finicky emperor who got a golden bed made. It was even fitted with lots of precious stones and diamonds. Whenever he had guests, he would offer the bed to them in the royal palace. The problem was, he had a rigid rule, had a certain mindset that the guests had to fit to the size of the bed. If the guests were a little taller, the emperor would cut them down to the size of the bed. The bed was so precious and valuable that it could not be altered, but the guests were altered according to the bed – it was as if the bed was not made for the guests but the guests had to be made as per the bed. It was very difficult, next to impossible actually, to find a man who could fit the bed as the bed was made after averaging the dimensions of the citizens. There were the youth, old people, short people, very tall people, children and women, so taking the average was hardly useful. They couldn't find a single person who was exactly the average height. So each guest was in deep trouble. If he was shorter than the bed, the emperor would call bodybuilders who would pull at the guests to try and fit them to the size of the bed. Eventually, each guest died but the emperor never deemed his deeds to be wrong. According to him, he was doing everything he could with the best intentions in the world.

When you have a certain mindset, despite all your good intentions, you will actually miss out on life because life is vast, not containable. You are trying to fit everything according to your mindset, metaphorically cutting many things and sometimes killing yourself and actually dying. Your mindset may cover certain angles but the tendency of the ego is to misrepresent its perspective as the whole. Now the problem is if you start wanting everything that is on your mind and claim that what you know is the whole then you will miss a connection with life. You will be blind to the realities. Your ego will trap you like a cocoon and you will be miserable. Then, in a bid to prove that we are not miserable, we start doing all the wrong things.

Similarly, you are trying to fit the people around you, your boss, your wife etc., as per your expectations. You are trying to fit almost everybody including yourself in the beliefs about everything you have in your mind. There is a mindset and you want everybody to fit in that mindset, even at the cost of cutting them to size and sometimes cutting yourself to size by even doing certain things to which your consciousness says no but you continue. You even want the situations in life to come as per your convenience. You want people to use words that please you.

You are totally absent to what is there because the ego is only conscious of what it wants.

Consciousness Technique

Whenever you are disturbed, instead of seeing who and what disturbed you, look deep inside of you, at the ever-expecting ego because of which you got disturbed. Only by dropping the screen of the past can one really see things. Otherwise the 'real you' inside is never given a chance, it is hidden under the old memories, the already trodden and the known. Are we playing with memories or the memories playing us?

Ego Keeps You Caged

Once in a village, there was a flood. Everybody was running helter-skelter to save their life. But the village priest, instead of trying to save his life, climbed a tree and sat at the top. The villagers asked him to go with them. He said, "No, God will come to save me. I have given my whole life for the service of God. I have full faith." After some time, the local police came and asked him to sit in their rescue boat. But he refused saying that he will go only with God. Now the water had almost reached his nose and half of the tree was under water.

Finally the last man came, the businessman of the village. He said, "Hey priest, I am the last one, you are very lucky, come quickly in the boat, you will be safe." But the priest refused repeating steadfastly that he will go only with God. After much cajoling, the businessman too went off, saving his own life. Now the water reached the top of the tree and the priest drowned and died. He went to God and complained, "Why the hell didn't you come to save me?" God said, "I came thrice. First in the disguise of the villagers, second as the police inspector and third as the businessman but you refused each time as you were caged in the knowledge you think you have that is really your ego." Life always offers you what you need; it just might not be in the same form. You search for a specific packaging, which the ego demanded, and forget to look at the content. Doing and happening are two different phenomenon altogether. God comes to us in various disguises and we search for him in stones and statues.

Ego Wants Attention

Ego wants importance and instead of letting you be a part of other people's worlds, it keeps you stuck in your own world, disconnecting you from others completely. When you are not present to what is happening, you miss connecting with people and life. People who are running after appreciation and attention are the biggest losers as others give you attention only when they get attention from you. Attention is given to attention and not to your personality, your intelligence, your money or your clout. So when you give attention, people return it. The whole society is running after respect, expecting it. Everybody wants respect but no one wants to give any. People feel if we give, then how will we get any? They think that if we always give respect then people will take us for granted and won't respect us. The problem is, everybody is waiting for the other person to talk to them first.

"Half the harm that is done in this world is due to people who want to feel important. They don't mean harm, but the harm that they cause is not visible or of interest to them either. They justify it because they are absorbed in the endless struggle of thinking well of themselves."

People keep gauging how important they are from the attention they get, forgetting that their value lies in how valuable they are for others.

Ego Wants, Consciousness Gives

Magic happens when you give respect even if just through the smallest gestures, with your eyes or maybe by standing up for someone when they come to meet you or holding the door for someone, listening attentively without judging, trying to be present in other people's worlds without expecting anything in return. The very act of giving respect amounts to giving respect to your own self. Wanting anything on the other hand makes you a beggar and keeps you anxious. When you give respect and importance to others, people want to be like you because you radiate charisma. One who gives will always be charismatic and one who wants will always be a beggar even if he is indisputably a king.

Complete Perception

When conscious, you become more aware and don't just perceive things on the basis of the belief systems created due to past experiences stored in the mind. You are aware of the present, your inner state and you perceive completely and wholly from what is right at the time of the situation and not what is right as per the programming of your mind. I remember when I was installing an air conditioner in my new flat; the estate manager told us to install the outside unit of the air conditioner on one of the windows and not on the terrace as someone might fiddle with it, the terrace being an open area. I had just started writing then and felt that if I put the air conditioner on my window, it will create noise and disturb me. At the time, I prioritised a silent working space above the safety of the air conditioner. I installed it on the terrace only and did not listen to the paranoid mind that was trying to threaten me with the consequences of what may happen. If I had functioned from the unaware mind, it would have been a fear-based reaction. I took action with my consciousness and installed it on the terrace. It is working fine.

In one of my training sessions, a young executive shared, "I had an amazing experience while doing my bachelor's degree. I was an average student but good at extra-curricular activities. I was a great singer. One day, a singing competition was held and I was the lead singer from my department. Although there were many good singers, I was not afraid. However, I spotted a singer representing another commerce faculty. This person was extremely good. I mean, he was amazing! After observing him, I lost my confidence because this guy seemed better than me.

After he performed, my name was announced. Suddenly, I did not feel prepared, as now I was conscious about his performance and ignorant about my abilities. I went on stage to sing, however, my mentor sensed my nervousness. He took hold of both my hands and said, 'You can do this. Just believe in yourself, because the only person standing in your way is your own ego making comparisons.' I moved forward with newfound determination and gave a great performance, I won that competition." Further, he shared, "I learned a very valuable lesson that day. I learned that no one can beat us unless we let them. Everything becomes right when we are present of our own unconsciousness."

The very awareness towards the impact of a reaction becomes the first step to consciousness and also the end of self-created suffering.

7

Ego Continues to Live in Complaining, Thinking & Comparing

Physical suffering is inevitable; accidents, diseases, old age and so on, but why has psychological suffering become a permanent feature of modern life too? Recently I fell off my cycle and hurt myself very badly, I was in massive pain. But now I don't remember the pain at all. Our brain often makes us forget our physical pain as a defence mechanism. But psychologically, the ego continuously nourishes the past emotional pain, hurt and hatred by sustaining the memory continuously, making us re-live it. If someone abused you ten years ago, your ego will remember it and will continue complaining, "Why did he abuse me?" throughout your life.

You cannot run away from where or who you are. You can only develop the power to handle your circumstances. It's important to develop this power as only *defying moments define you.*

Ego's Habit of Complaining & Criticising

Recently a friend's sister got married. My friend, over the phone, complained to me, "When we came out of the dressing room with the bride, my sister's future brother-in-law said that the bride was not looking so good, even though in my opinion, she was looking great. See how inconsiderate the boy's family is? Instead of praising my sister, they criticized her." While my friend was talking, I immediately recognised that her ego had taken over because of the ego's tell-tale and persistent habit of complaining about people and situations. I knew that she does the same thing usually – she either complains about herself or others. Now to the consciousness, it's not important whether my friend's sister was actually looking good or not, but for the ego, it is. When you don't complain, you can deal with *what is* instead of mentally struggling with what *it* should not be.

Ego Doesn't Allow One to Take Responsibility

I knew it was her ego that was making her avoid taking responsibility. This is the ego's strategy because it doesn't want to address the complaint and by complaining, it shifts the blame onto something or someone else. Her ego was making the complaint sound so real that she, too, believed it. When egos are empty and don't have much else to identify with, they survive on complaining. I asked my friend, "What did you say to your sister's brother-in-law who said that the bride is not looking good?" She said, "We all felt very bad and I told him in a sharp tone that this is not the way to behave but instead of listening to me, he left and said, 'People can't tolerate the truth.'"

The moment you talk to someone sharply, abuse someone

verbally, or even just feel like shouting at them, know for sure that the ego has taken over you. The ego then starts pretending to be you and starts reacting. All this complaining makes you feel bitter as you continue thinking about other people's wrongs. Whatever you keep thinking about and ponder upon, becomes the inclination of your consciousness and your vibrations are coloured by the same, so you can choose between creating more negativity and a free-flowing positivity.

I asked my friend how this incident made her feel. She said, "Drained… and the brother-in-law is also avoiding us now." She felt drained because the ego keeps judging and evaluating what others do, what they do not do, how wrong and right it is, etc.

I told my friend, "There are many possibilities as to why he said that but instead of judging him, take this as an opportunity to work on yourself." One of the ways of dealing with situations like these is, firstly, to understand that other people too are controlled by their ego as you are. Secondly, many times the faults that you see in others are a result of your projection and wrong interpretation. Thirdly, if somebody hurts us, chances are, he may be getting hurt by us, consciously or unconsciously. We fail to see what is driving other people's behaviour because we are not aware of their world. It's very important to take note of the unsaid communication that takes place all the time through people's tone, words, gestures, comments and behaviour to know where they are coming from. Complaining is a way of avoiding having to handle things.

Ego Justifies its Actions

My friend started justifying herself by saying things like, *"Trust me, I know,"* and *"Why do you never trust me."* Your ego keeps justifying the acts it forces upon you as being right and labels whatever others do as wrong if not in consonance with its programming. Justifying itself as right makes the ego feel superior to others.

You might actually be right in many discussions but when you assert yourself with force, that's the ego's doing. You may be right, but the forceful and adamant justifications spoil the whole thing and people are taken aback. You can state a fact without imposing the "me" in it on others. Just avoid taking things personally. If the population of the world is 7.6 billion then there are 7.6 billion realities. The problem with the ego is that it falsely assumes that what is real to it is the truth.

The ego justifies its position or attacks people when they blame, disagree with or infringe upon your decisions, or make you answerable for a mishap or the way you handled a particular situation. During such times it becomes more important for the ego to justify than being calm. Observe the aggressive energy that starts rushing inside you, making you angry. The best way to catch the ego in the act is through your own voice that becomes rough, sharp, high, low and sometimes silent when trying to justify or force an outcome.

Ask yourself this: who are you protecting when you are justifying yourself? The ego. It cannot accept that it can go wrong. Ego is this self-protecting entity that can only see and accept what it knows. When you are present, the force with which you talk and justify your acts will disappear, you will be filled with humility. When you are a hollow man, with no ego inside, you don't get hurt. *Only the ego hurts and gets hurt.* The moment you start to justify your actions, the defence mechanism of the mind is switched on.

The purpose of the mind is to identify how it will handle the future using past knowledge. That's the way we do our daily functions. The problem arises when we don't want the mind's services but it continues as the off button is not found. So it is always active, giving suggestions to handle the future and when it does not have anything for the future, it keeps trying to mend the past. Notice, in our mind, either we keep repeating an old thought or worry about the future. This working of the mind disturbs our conscious energy as it creates inner conflicts and consumes intelligence till the time the off button is found. The off button exists, and it is consciousness, it is awareness. The moment you are aware, the mind stops.

When we learn to be present, we can keep the mind aside when it is not in use. The mind does not have a choice; it will not be able to react. Consciousness is choice. The problem is never making the right or wrong decision; it's about losing your inner power which is the source of how you feel and live.

Once the inner power is lost, the centre is lost, no matter how much money you have, you will feel shaky and under confident. And whatever work you do after losing your inner power, the quality of your performance will go down. When the quality goes down, the mind justifies its actions to others and to yourself, stating that you are right and it is the situation which is wrong and in doing so you lose the opportunity to grow and learn.

When something goes wrong, instead of choosing the ego, you can choose consciousness and be aware of the inner dialogue, feelings and intentions as much as you are aware of the outside situations and what people say.

Getting Lost in the Complaint

The moment I started giving my friend (the one I spoke about earlier in this chapter) advice, she started providing me evidence about how bad the people from the boy's side really were and very angrily said that she will show them what she is made of. Some egos even feel that their complaint is so legitimate, they try to get proof to support it. She started telling me specific instances to show that her complaint was valid and even told me to talk to her father so that I could get the facts verified and agree with her. I told her, "This will make you feel even more right and will keep you 'trapped' in the complaint. It's better not to defend yourself."

Ego is Impatient

The moment you catch yourself having thoughts of revenge, hurting someone, being hurt, wanting to give it back to people, or taking an aggressive decision, just wait for 24 hours. Drop that thought for 24 hours and then see what happens. Majority of the time the aggression vanishes; just don't do what the ego suggests. Stopping the ego's chatter is an act of consciousness.

I gave an example to my friend and said, "Not complaining does not mean listening to what is not appropriate or bearing poor quality of work. There is no ego in telling the caterer that the sweet dish is not up to the mark if you stick to the facts." Her complaining was negative because when you say, "How dare you serve this food to my guests..." There is a "me" that feels personally offended by the bad food, as if it was done on purpose. I told her that she similarly took it personally when the brother-in-law said that her sister was not looking good. Of course, many egos also enjoy making someone wrong but if you are aware, you become invincible and don't get hurt. But if you try to be invulnerable, you make a wall around you and get all the more hurt. So it's important you stay vulnerable, that is, open to hurt but being aware. Then no one can hurt you. You can be defeated only if you are willing to win. In awareness winning or losing is not the question but living lovingly is.

Change Causes Persistence

Trying to change the other person or the negative thoughts that you have doesn't work in real life. You try to think positive on the seeds of the negative, causing even more confusion and misery. However, no change has the power to make your emotions disappear. Whatever you try to change gets even more firmly established and takes hold of you. Consciously just choose to be the way you want to be, inventing new possibilities instead of changing. For example, if you want to stop being angry, instead of changing that aspect of your behaviour, start loving. Instead of changing, create what is possible; with nothing to fix, no place to get to, and no results to achieve, you experience freedom from changing and feel alive. Complaining usually leaves us with complacency, doubt, resignation and tiredness. There is no room left for other points of view that can inspire, enliven or make a positive difference. Complaints are not bad or wrong; they just lead to a life that is different from a life full of power, freedom, and self-expression.

Don't try to remove the ego, but don't expand it either by brooding over things. Those are negative emotions.

Let things be there in your egoistic mind. They won't disturb you, if you don't support them with your attention and, or identify with them.

The worst thing about complaining is that it is always going to make you angry and upset. Forgiving people and forgetting such thoughts removes the emotional charge of the complaint that keeps strengthening the ego. This charge contains the bitterness that makes you a victim. The ego majorly sustains itself by reliving the past, being its victim and trying to be a victor. If the ego doesn't understand the deeper meaning hidden behind what happened, its whole view gets coloured, changing the way you talk and behave. Ego takes a hold of you and not only starts ruining your relationships but also impacts your work, health, peace of mind and keeps you stressed.

The ego, once triggered, starts telling us to go ahead of our friends, neighbours, conquer and win everything and we start pushing ourselves, not seeing what is currently happening and where exactly our attention is needed. Maybe your boss is giving you a clue that he is not happy with you but your attention is on the complaint, "Why didn't the boss give me a raise?" Be wise and understand what his behaviour towards you means. This is the easiest way of shedding the ego. Don't justify your mistakes or resist things, otherwise you will remain stuck in the ego and appear very childish, too. There may be old complaints but every time you catch your ego complaining, it weakens and over a period of time it starts to disappear.

There may be old complaints but every time you catch your ego complaining, it weakens and over a period of time starts to disappear.

Don't try to shove away things by saying, "I don't have any complaints." Be authentic and watch – are you aggressive majority of the times? Do you stay tired? Do you keep judging people, and are you too critical? If so, then you are harbouring a complaint. Often we see ourselves as we want to be and not how we actually are.

You don't get energy by just attending a seminar or reading a book. All our capabilities, competence and abilities flow through this energy. And when I found the energy, instead of wasting it on settling scores and partying, I started using it to work on my ego. Energy increases capabilities and the same situations that initially looked colossal start looking minuscule.

Handling Complaints

The process to look at complaints:

- Wherever you are, look at your life and see what you are resisting; situations that you should deal with but try to avoid. Look at something that you are putting up with; things that you don't want to do but do out of compulsion. Look at what you are avoiding; like resolving a relationship problem, work- or health-related issues. Look at what you are trying to fix and change; maybe your wife speaks a lot and you want to change that or your boss or friends don't care about you and you want them to care.

- Identify how you react when the person does the impugned act.

- Look at the impact that the complaining has on you.

- Who do you have to complain about in that situation? What do you have to say about that person?

For example, the complaint I had with almost all my friends was that no one spoke to me about the issues I was going through. They gave me money when I had none, but I felt left out. I wanted to say that my friends were not involved in my world. They were the only lifeboat I had after separating from my family, that too without money.

My complaint was that my friends were not present for me emotionally when I got separated from my family; I neither had a place to stay nor any job. I had no one in life except them and I got so scared and worried that just within 30 days of fighting with the family I developed thyroid. I had also separated from my girlfriend, though we patched-up later. I did not have as many complaints with my own family as I had with my friends. I wanted to change them but soon I realised that my expecting ego had shielded the reality from me and it took me, lot of courage to confront it and see the reality. I addressed my ego by having a conversation with it, by becoming totally aware of its movements.

Earlier, whenever I met my friends, I was just putting up with them and wasn't really comfortable because in the background the complaint switch was always on. I avoided confronting it for a long time. Then I tried to change my friends by telling them that they didn't give me emotional support when I was struggling in life after separating from my father, even though they supported me with whatever they could. They were not too comfortable with this as they had done everything that I required at that time. One friend lent me his flat to stay at for almost a fortnight, two friends gave me their places to start my centre, two gave me the initial down payment to pay for my new house, one gave me an air-conditioner and the rest gifted me with a TV, microwave oven, computer and mobile phone for the housewarming ceremony of the new place I had bought.

When I became aware of the impact that my complaints were having over me, I sat down and made a list of all the help my friends extended to me and opened the eyes of my blind ego, which does not see what it gets but only sees what it expects. I realised that they were all present but I didn't ask for what I wanted. If I wanted emotional support I could have called them, visited them or asked them to visit. This clarity got me out of the complaining mode and also helped me access my consciousness. I used this stressful situation to produce calm energy and used it to write this book. You need support when you are weak and you ask for support when you are strong, irrespective of the consequences. On the contrary, when you are internally strong, balanced and calm, people around you support you without your asking. You get all the support needed, as your consciousness itself is working inside of you naturally. When you become natural and go with the life's flow, you too flow and cross obstacles without getting hurt. But when your ego is active and resistant, even a pebble becomes a hurdle in your path. The gist is, instead of getting egoistic and waiting for others to come to you, go and express what you want with awareness that will keep your energy positive and not make them negative.

The moment you become aware of the complaining at the thought and emotional level, as felt by your body, you will realise that YOU are not complaining, it's the habitual mind pattern of the ego. Complaints arise when the ego is threatened. You can accept anything when you are present, that is, free from the ego. When you are aware there are no complaints, just opportunities to look within and grow.

To drop the "I" you have to be with "them".

Breaking the Ego's Language with Love

Language is a beautiful tool to become aware. Normally egocentric people use the language of logic, but this logic is as per their perception. The language of logic is always argumentative. It does not believe in discussions but rather in proving that it is right and the other is wrong. Anybody who indulges in justifications will become aggressive and violent. Such people will always try to convince other people. Their whole thrust is upon seeing who is right and who is wrong instead of seeing what is right. Such egocentric persons are not concerned with other people but only with their own egos. When you talk in the language of logic, connecting with people is difficult and you remain confined to connecting only with your "type" of people.

If a girl says "I love you" to a person who operates only on logic, he might start asking questions – "Why do you love me? "Why do you want to marry me?" and so on. He won't even know what love is and therefore, live a dry life throughout. A man in love may say that his wife's face is like the moon and a person who is too logical will contradict it by saying the husband is crazy, the moon is so big and his wife's face is so small. He is unable to see the poetry in the expression.

In the language of love, you are not concerned with your ego but with the other person. Moreover, you don't have an ego. You are not important at all, your priority is to make the other person feel important. There is no reason, no logic but to help the other grow, transform, feel cared for and respected. And this is not to score points, which would again hint at the ego, but it's genuine care. In the language of logic, what is said is important but in the language of love, how it is said is important. That's why people with an aggressive demeanour are never their boss' favourite. They are so unconscious that instead of correcting their behaviour, they justify it. People treat you the way you train them to treat you. Because of their unruly and rude behaviour, their bosses too get trained to treat them the same way. They keep justifying their wrong behaviour by lying to themselves, saying, "The work I do is important and not the way I talk or behave."

In the language of love, not the words but the meaning and feeling behind the words are more important. So even if someone is using a wrong word, but he does so out of love, he will be accepted and loved back. Whereas a person who always talks in the language of logic might be talking sense but if his way is not that of love, it will be rejected. The language of love is always communicated heart-to-heart, that's why even when our friends talk to us using abusive language, it doesn't hurt us. As a matter of fact, when they don't talk in that manner, it's a sign that something is wrong.

Love does not even need forgiveness. Still, forgive the ones who have hurt you. They didn't know what they were doing. They were unconscious just as you were or are. Forgiveness also gives clarity of action to the one who has been forgiven and the fruits of introspection to the one who forgives. If you carry a grudge against anybody, your whole being will be impacted and so will your relationships. The ego's inner instinct is to punish and reprimand, whereas consciousness forgives people and kindles forgiveness in them. Today the world is a

The moment you think of getting even with people, your mind will start telling you what to do and disturb you even further.

mess just because of our inability to forgive each other, share and care for one another. This is the source of our misery. When you forgive people, you are alive. When you forgive, your ego stops the incessant suggestions that it otherwise keeps sending about how to hurt someone who hurt you, to seek revenge.

So finally, I told my friend to forgive the brother-in-law who had passed an unkind comment on the bride for not looking attractive and she did and felt relieved from the stress.

The problem is, we become the complaint and then our hatred communicates with people. I learnt not to be afraid of expressing strong emotions. Many a times they won't be taken in the right spirit. Still express, learn what makes people feel bad and next time change your ways. The insight itself is liberating, the rest is just perfunctory.

We don't get stressed by what people do, but from what we do with the information we glean from their actions. The moment you have thoughts of reconciliation, the disturbing ego shuts down itself. The moment you think of getting even with people, your mind will start telling you what to do and disturb you even further. These instructions received from the ego are stressful. Forgiving the wrongs of others is maturity.

Forgiving others after understanding that what they did was

right from their point of view will keep your mind relaxed. A relaxed mind has the requisite creative energy to resolve things. Then you have the power to go and talk to people if you find they did something that was not right. So don't interrupt people when they are expressing something, so that the ego cannot create tension in you and in them. This way you can ease out beforehand, successfully avoiding what the ego would have got you into. When you are relaxed, nothing can disturb you. When you are tensed, nothing can calm you except your own volition to do so. Getting out of the complaining mode and actually talking from the perspective of a healing mode is what makes us present and free from the ego. This also gives rest to the tired mind.

Learning Instead of Complaining & Blaming

I remember having a fight with a boss of mine who was very high on integrity. I had struck a tie-up in Nepal to open a marketing centre there for our courses when I was working with a college. I convinced our counterparts there to pay 50 per cent of the advertising cost to gather students for the various courses we offered. I went to my boss, excited to tell him the news. When I told him about the tie-up, he said that he is interested in opening the marketing wing only if the counterpart pays 100 per cent of the advertising money. I said, "This can't be done, as I have already confirmed payment of 50 per cent of the advertising cost and now rescinding will shake their trust in us and make him question our integrity." My boss said this is the integrity we owe to our business, as times change one should keep sufficient margin to go back and forth on a few commitments. If you keep the margin then there is integrity. He told me to renegotiate. To my astonishment, when I spoke to our Nepalese counterpart he agreed to pay full advertising costs, of course after some initial resistance. I learnt from business that at times you have to be flexible and reconsider things, especially if you have a boss, and this is actually good as there is always a cushion to fall back upon. So it's better to tell the person involved on the other end that final confirmation will come from the boss alone. Problems arise mostly when you get too logical and fail to see the practical side of things. Intelligence is required to see where to be logical, where to be emotional and where to go beyond both.

There are people who gather experience, and learn and there are some who keep adding to their frustrations and complaints.

Being Appreciative

Being genuinely appreciative and expressing the same helps you enhance the presence of consciousness in you and drop your ego. We forget to appreciate what others are doing for us and keep seeing what they are not doing, what we are not getting in life, and what we don't like. When you appreciate people they open up and there is self-expression. In this self-expression, a space gets created for you to be accepted by them as well. Attention to its chatter is what the ego craves. You can only appreciate life and people when you ignore the ego's never-ending complaints. The ego's habitual pattern of complaining starts to lose grip when the message 'I am not interested in what you are saying' gets communicated to it loud and clear.

Ego Makes You a 'Thinking Addict'

Thoughts have their own use but 80 to 90 per cent of people's thinking actually consists of a phenomenon that can be called "thoughting". When doing this, they are not entirely aware and the automated pilot mode keeps traversing through a spiral of thoughts, "He said this, why did he say that, he should not have said it, why does this happen to me only, why do only I suffer" and so on.

> **Being present is being the pilot. Do not allow the mind to run you. Instead, you run it.**

When you switch off this auto-mode and see situations as they are, you can think. Seeing without judging is observing. Observation then gives way to thinking. When you are able to think about what you want to do consciously, action comes out as a natural result of self-expression. Being aware helps you not get addicted to 'thoughting', which you feel is thinking. If you identify yourself with thoughts, chances are you will be a "thinking addict", and there are no rehabilitation centres to get you free from this addiction. Asylums only keep your bodies when your mind roams free on its destructive path.

This addiction to thinking, right from the childhood, paves the way for your personality. *As a "thinking addict", you don't have a point of view but rather you become your point of view.*

When you identify with something, your personality becomes egocentric; you may have identified with money, respect, an idea, an opinion or even attention. There is no place for acceptance in the lives of egocentric personalities. They come across as arrogant, but in the true sense they are what they have attached themselves to and will always try to protect their mental image. Such people keep justifying their actions, their behaviour and even their sense of self their whole life. The very nature of the ego is such that it cannot live in the present moment. As its major function is to justify things, it keeps justifying the past and lives in an imagined future, causing insecurity and anxiety. They become control freaks. When you talk to them, you can very easily see that such people only talk about themselves, criticise others and presume that their intellect is superior.

There is a Japanese bird which flees a town twenty-four hours before an earthquake. Our scientists, on the other hand, are not able to predict it even two hours in advance. Human beings possess this inner sense too but have lost the ability by using the mind, the intellect excessively. When our inner vision, which can look beyond words and situations, starts to develop, we will have access to that kind of intelligence, too.

Know Your Future

What you will become tomorrow is connected to what you are doing today. If you notice, you will see that whatever happens tomorrow is in some way predictable even today. So if your mind keeps using the past to create the future, things will keep repeating. Whereas if you live in the present moment, you will observe that whatever is in the process has already occurred. The future is not utterly uncertain, our knowledge is uncertain. Nothing from the future is revealed to you because you are blind. And because nothing of the future is revealed to you, you say it is uncertain. Look closely, when you are reacting rudely to your boss, or your wife, you are already sowing seeds for future fights.

Let your life and your work do the talking.

The Comparing Ego

One of the major indicators that we are being operated by the ego is the dreadful affliction of comparison. When you compare yourself, notice that it is always with someone who you think is better than you. So when you compare, you are trying to be someone else and not who you are, otherwise there is no need to do it. You keep rejecting yourself in the race to be the best by being someone else, you keep living in an illusion; instead of being the best you, you try to be the best version of others, which only creates conflict within you. This conflict does not allow you to capitalize on your strengths and the ego keeps trying to be someone else, making you lose your power.

Only a mind free of the ever-comparing ego can experience bliss. If you don't compare, can you be unintelligent or dumb? You are less only when you compare. Now, think for a minute, how will a dull mind think, work and relate with people? In a dull way, right? So if you don't compare, what is available to you? Your intelligence will be available to you, which is neither dull nor sharp. It is pure intelligence and absolutely uninfluenced by comparison, available completely at your disposal, to use the way you want to use it. Notice ego derives its confidence from comparison. When the ego says "I am the best", it's coming from comparison as you can only be the best in reference to someone. The moment you prove yourself right, you have wronged the other person. And nobody likes to be "wronged", to be on the receiving end. Our habit of proving others wrong comes from the psychological need of wanting to be better. Once you have proved the other wrong, he too tries to prove himself right by wronging you. Our lives cease but this game of one-upping never ends.

One can cultivate new attitudes by dropping the comparison. What people have, get or/and do is none of your concern. Focus on your life and what you have. If there is labour and hard work in your life then you might as well enjoy it, because if you love what you have then you have what you love, but if you don't love what you have you still have it and you suffer. True competition is not to defeat the other but to win other people's hearts. If need be, after completing your work, help others. This way you will truly win by reaching your whole potential, utilising your hidden talents and creativity, not just working for the boss, money or company but giving it your fullest. When you give your full, you automatically fulfil the expectations of your seniors and earn much more than what you earn by trying to run away from work or having an aggressive demeanour. The same goes for husbands who can help their wives with home chores. There is nothing noble about being superior to your fellow men. True nobility lies in being superior to your former self. Just do the work as it comes and also do in advance the work that you can foresee.

Planning and strategizing well will always help you save time. I complete my work at airport lounges while waiting for my flights and when I reach home I am free to do what I want to do. As a matter of fact, I get more time to work and complete as much as I can when I travel. I want "Used Up" to be written on my epitaph. I want to live life burning from both the ends. Each moment should be filled with action and not just be a reaction to old complaints. Stress arises when you know certain things should be done and you still don't do them. No stress means peace and performance. Once I had to submit an important proposal to a company, I finished my work on the flight itself and to my surprise, when I reached home there was no electricity. I didn't only save time but also the pressure that would have mounted due to incomplete work till the electricity was restored. Ordinary people who are run by their egos keep making up excuses, "I couldn't complete the work as there was no electricity", whereas people who are aware get insights that make them proactive, something inside them keeps telling and guiding them.

Give everything your best, even if it is just in your own eyes.

Don't do it to show anyone or the boss. People automatically come to know when you have given your best. And who cares whether they come to know or not. You should know that you are giving your best. So work with this resolution, there is no fear the moment you resolve that NOTHING IS IMPOSSIBLE. Know your duties and your rights will be taken care of. If you have given your best, you won't feel bad. You only feel bad when you leave some stones unturned. Your goals and the company's goal should align so that separation becomes impossible. Confidence and knowledge about your abilities come when you do something that is difficult. Let your work do the talking. When you drop what you are not, what you are emerges. Beyond hatred, violence and anger is love and compassion. The closer you get to your natural self and farther from the egoistic self, the more confident you feel. Hesitation comes when you try to be something that you are not.

Ego is a Price Tag

I recently met an acquaintance at a restaurant. She asked me where I was staying as I had shifted from my old residence. Then after having a small chat, she invited all of us for dinner, unknowingly adding that they had recently constructed a mansion on 30,000 square feet of land. Notice how the ego becomes a "price tag". Its design is to equate *having more* with *being happy*.

One of my uncles had a huge factory. Whenever I would visit him, he would show me the entire factory and derive tremendous pleasure out of it. Now, I had visited his factory more than ten times but still he would take me around as if showing it to me for the first time. This one time I observed that he appeared sad. I asked my auntie what had happened, she said in the same cheerful tone as before, "Didn't you notice the new factory next to us, which is bigger than ours?" Now, auntie is the same as before, full of energy, but my uncle was dejected because of his habit of comparing. The new factory in the neighbourhood had made his factory old.

The Trap of Respectability

Are you trying to satisfy some psychological need? Do you feel internally at peace with who you are, bereft of your material possessions? Can you determine your own value or are you always depending on others to put a tag on you, on your values and evaluate you? If so, you are trapped.

How do you buy anything – a car, house, clothes? Majority of the people who have not found their own remote control for their moods, feelings and emotions compulsively show off and crave getting attention and importance from other people. That's what keeps their egos satiated till the dose from other people lasts. We have been conditioned to gather material things, earn a name and some fame. We have been given enough evidence to convince us that if we don't earn respect, we won't be accepted by people and the society and will be left alone and lonely. You also experience the same when you get down from your small car and your friend says, "Idiot, why have you got the small car, don't you know it's downmarket?" He also says that wearing a Rolex will make you feel confident and earn respect.

Once when we were going to a function at the lakeside, a reunion lunch, one of my friends said, "I think we should wear formal clothes," as he was in a casual shirt and jeans. The weather was not cold; there was a very pleasant breeze, the kind that blows right before the winters. I told him, "Imagine if the present principal comes in shorts and a t-shirt saying, 'Hi guys!', then what will you do?"

We are so conditioned to follow what we know that we can't even see what's right for us given the present situation. We keep looking at life from the aspect of what should be, instead of what is. Our whole life just passes by and we keep figuring out what is right and what is wrong, missing out on life in the battle of right versus wrong.

The problem is that no one is interested in the real you, they only look at your clothes, the outer surface, your exterior.

Many people who have succeeded in achieving all the material wealth of the world continue to complain about still being insecure, guilty, scared and competitive. They remain in a negative inner state despite going through such rigour to achieve all the success. So how do all those achievements help in living a great life? Externally yes, it awards you with physical comforts, people's appreciation, respect, etc., but is this respect for who you are as a human being, or for the material possessions you have? Deep inside, you are still feeling diffident, anxious, depressed and sad as all the attention and love you get from people is for what you have and not for who you are. So eventually, what you sought from the achievements is still missing and is making you even more miserable. Earning respect by selling yourself and buying expensive clothes is not a good idea. It is only because people show that they are happy running after money that we get disillusioned. The moment someone tries showing that he is happy, know that he is suffering and suppressing the suffering through the show of pleasure, calling it happiness.

Jealousy Comes from Comparison

Are we getting people's love by buying bigger houses or are we attracting their jealousy? When you share, you get love, but do we share our achievements or use them to cover our inferiority complexes? Right from our childhood our parents compare us to the neighbours' children, with our cousins, our peers. Right from then, we spend our whole life comparing because someone will always have a prettier bungalow, a more chiselled body, a better personality or an overflowing bank account. The outcome is always jealousy, a by-product of comparison.

When you get centred in your consciousness and out of the conditioned ego, jealousy simply evaporates. You come to the understanding that you are you and it is stupid to compare, as everybody is original not at all comparable unless you want to be and live like carbon copies.

A restaurant owner was complaining to his neighbour about the tsunami and how it washed away almost everything that he had. The neighbour, trying to be sympathetic, said, "Oh my God, your whole restaurant and the kitchen is washed down the stream."

"How about Venkat's restaurant?" asked the restaurant owner.

The neighbour said, "It's gone, too"

"And Swami's?"

"His too."

"Humph!" said the owner who had lost everything, with a grin, "It isn't as bad as I thought."

If other people are also suffering, then it is acceptable for the ego. If others are happy and moving ahead in life, the ego feels pathetic. If everybody is losing, the ego feels good. Thoughts about "others" are a warning sign that you have not allowed your own consciousness to flow; you have not allowed your own bliss to grow, you have not allowed yourself to bloom. Hence you feel empty inside, and you look at each and everybody's life superficially because you can only see the outside. Internally we know how miserable we feel without our possessions and achievements. The ego sees other people's big bungalows, cars and dresses and feels jealous. In the same way others know how miserable they feel inside and see only your outside, creating jealousy in their minds. Everybody's charade is very beautiful. Our exteriors are mere showpieces and they are meant to deceive. We get deceived as we are not happy on the inside.

Many times you pretend to have things that you don't have. I remember, after our split from the S. Kumar's group, one of my friends came to drop me home. Instead of getting down in front of my house, I got down at my neighbour's as it was well-maintained in comparison to our worn-out and lacklustre home. I was just 12 years old then. Even at such a young age you start pretending to have things you can't have, trying to be what you can't be. You become more and more fake while copying others. Jealousy is hell and when you feel discomfort on the inside, you can't let go of it. But jealousy can be dropped right now, if you drop the habit of comparing. The moment you stop comparing, all the diseases that were brought about by being fake will disappear too.

Ego's Beauty Comes from its Conditioning

What is beautiful to the ego can become ugly the very next moment as what it considers to be beautiful does not come from your essence, your deep core. Ego's sense of beauty comes from what it has been made to believe. That's why they say, "Beauty lies in the eyes of the beholder." People who are having the presence of the divine, the consciousness, will see beauty everywhere, even in what appears ugly to the rest. Because consciousness does not derive beauty from outside but keeps experiencing it by itself. A man who is awakened definitely values aesthetics and beauty but at the same time does not hanker for it.

Considered a mark of beauty in the Mursi tribe of Ethiopia, Africa, the lip plate is worn by women daily to seek acceptance and to appear desirable to men. When the women are ready to marry, they begin the process of putting on the lip plate by making a hole in the lower lip with a wooden stick, which is expanded a little every day. Eventually, when the hole is big enough, women insert a plate and gradually a bigger plate replaces the earlier plate until it has reached its full size. It is a very painful process girls have to undergo for months, sometimes teeth have to be broken to insert the plate, but once succeeded, they are seen as the epitome of beauty! It is believed that the bigger the plate, the more beautiful the woman.

The plate is usually a sacred object, dyed and decorated according to the wearer's preferences. Women are also shaved, like the men, because they don't like hair.

Are you ugly now? No one is ugly if there is no comparison.

Comparison Destroys Self Love

In one of my training programs, I met a young executive who said that he couldn't accept his body as he thought he was fat. I told him he is fat because he is comparing; how otherwise can he be fat? He has an image of a slim body in his mind, maybe of a film star and his ego tells him, "Look, this is called a perfect body, you are not like this." When I saw him, he was absolutely okay and as a matter of fact, a handsome man too. But he was unnecessarily anxious and suffering because of a few extra kilos around his waistline. He felt that nobody loved him because he was fat. Now this comparison was making him lose his whole life. Because of this comparison, he cannot love and won't allow anybody to love him. If someone showed interest in him, he would think, "How can anybody love me, I am unlovable," as he does not love his own self. So whosoever will love him, he will think that person is in it for his money or for some other ulterior motive.

You can't trust anybody when you doubt yourself.

Ego and False Ambition

Comparison also makes one falsely ambitious. Today the majority is suffering because of the ambition that is fuelled by their egos, a soulless ambition which is not created by knowing one's own core skill set, passion or purpose in life. This ego-based ambition only brings competition with one another. And where there is competition, there will be comparison and where there is comparison there is suffering.

Observe: a mind that is free from comparison is available to move in the direction you put it to. There is no illusion left and one can create whatever one wants rather than just trying to be someone else or seeing what others are getting and how much they are enjoying.

If the approach of collecting wealth is failing to give us a holistic life, then why don't we take a completely different approach? We have been to the moon and back successfully but psychologically speaking, we are just the same with the same misery and pain. Honestly answer yourself, "Are you truly happy?" If not, then you have the wrong definition and the wrong method of being happy. The definition that your mind has is very different from what gives happiness. If you are suffering, whatever you are doing to be happy will be momentary and will again and again put you through a vicious cycle of pleasure and pain, trying to create past experiences and pleasures over and over again, sometimes by thinking and sometimes by repeating, expecting.

8

Ego & Happiness

Happiness is not about gathering things but about holding yourself together on the inside, unbroken, unfragmented, undivided and "unwanting". You cannot experience happiness by getting something, but by getting rid of all the things that make you sad. People who are searching for happiness through name and fame from the world outside are bound to suffer because they are looking at material things, demanding favourable conditions matching the rules and list of wants that they have written in their minds. They are living a conditional life. If their conditions get fulfilled, they might get happy, if not, they wait for them to be fulfilled. *This waiting and wanting constitute endless suffering.* It is by default the way it is. Another problem with desiring material objects is that even before one desire gets fulfilled, the race for the next begins. It's a vicious cycle that never ends. This is because all these desires are not yours. They are listed by your egoistic mind. So even if they are fulfilled you feel deprived and dissatisfied.

In this limited material world and in the domain of the limited and conditioned mind, you are looking for unlimited happiness from temporary things.

You see everybody running after success and feel this is how things are supposed to be. This is how the world is. Somewhere you start ignoring the other side of things, where people around you are also stressed, frustrated and unhappy. Since you are blind to your own sufferings you cannot see it in others as well.

Opening the Inner Eye

It is so easy to see one person feeling happy when he gets a raise and the other when he gets praised. One may get happiness in going on an adventure trip; the other may feel happy meditating. One may feel happy being with friends and the other might enjoy solitude. So where exactly is happiness? If you have been unhappy till now, what will guarantee your happiness in the future? Will changing the object of your desire make any difference to your feelings? If you require anything to be happy then you cannot be happy, you can have pleasure but not happiness. Happiness is a state of your consciousness. Ego gets motivated with things, consciousness is motivation.

What Makes You Happy?

Everything you choose is coming from an attitude and new attitudes are formed on the basis of what you choose. When you try to derive happiness from a source other than your inner states, you start becoming dependent. Very soon you will notice whatever gave you happiness will also make you sad later on. Why, because that pleasure you felt, which you thought was happiness, led you to expect happiness the next time as well. You get stuck in a vicious circle of pleasure, desire and suffering. Now you keep doing the same activity trying to repeat earlier the experience of the past.

Slowly and slowly the ability to recreate your feelings by changing your thoughts or being without thoughts diminishes because the neuro-plasticity of the brain declines with age. Neuro-plasticity alters pathways in the neural wiring of the brain with the help of thoughts and emotions. These pathways trigger our actions and behaviours.

We contact people and acquire objects in order to be happy. When a certain desire is fulfilled, the ego temporarily becomes calm that results in a flash of happiness within. But not realising the fact that the happiness that we experienced was from within, we start correlating our feelings with the objects. We become convinced that it was the object that made us happy and get attached to it. The more the joy is superimposed, the greater the attachment. This causes dependence, possessiveness, jealousy and fear leading to sorrow, tension and agitation. Having derived imagined happiness from objects and people, we remain bound by our attachment. Moreover, we also experience the law of diminishing returns – most things that we imagine to be "pleasurable" over a period of time turn out to be less so despite of their remaining constant. For instance, the satisfaction derived from one glass of wine when we were in our early twenties or a new car that we bought two years ago won't be same today. It diminishes. Only when this false notion is consciously destroyed can the mind become unattached and free.

Consciousness Technique

Stop seeking; tell the ego that you don't want people's attention or appreciation. The rushing ego will stop and with it the need for respect too will cease. When you don't seek, you are present, you are whole.

The mind is a very faithful servant who follows clear instructions. When the ego stops rushing, the mind's quick thinking too stops automatically. It is quick because it always works under fear, to fulfil the ego's expectations as quickly as possible and get over with its work. So after relaxing the mind by not working for a while and giving it some time, the mind becomes calmer and is capable of functioning better.

Buddha was once travelling with a few of his followers. As they were passing a lake, Buddha told one of his disciples, "I am thirsty. Do get me some water from the lake." The disciple walked up to the lake. At that moment, a bullock cart began crossing through the lake. As a result, the water became very muddy and turbid. The disciple thought, "How can I give this muddy water to Buddha to drink?"

So he came back and told Buddha, "The water in there is very muddy. I don't think it is fit to drink." After about half an hour, again Buddha asked the same disciple to go back to the lake. The disciple went back, and found that the water was still muddy. He returned and informed Buddha about it. After sometime, Buddha asked the same disciple to go back again. This time, the disciple found that the mud had settled down, and the water was clean and clear. So he collected some water in a pot and brought it to Buddha. Buddha looked at the water, and then he looked up at the disciple and said, "See what did you do to make the water clean? You let it be and the mud settled down on its own, and you have clear water."

Your ego is like that, too! When it is disturbed, just let it be. Give it a little time, it will settle down on its own. You don't have to put in any effort to calm it down. It will happen. It is effortless.

When fully present/conscious, I even feel like meeting the people who hurt me in the past. When I am disturbed, I try to avoid even those who love me in the present.

Keep calming your energy. Initially just observe the egoistic energy, don't try to change the thoughts as changing is the action of the ego. It's important to observe how our mind works in order to transform it.

The absence of incessant thoughts implies the presence of relaxation. Whatever you achieve in the material world can be enjoyed only when you are relaxed. The ability to stay relaxed is the greatest power. Ego-based power is destructive and will always keep you uneasy. Once you get present to this real power that comes from being aware, your life will become smooth and easy and you will have greater potential and determination to achieve your material goals and live a holistic life. The secret is – minimizing thoughts by being attentive and eventually reaching a point where only attention is left. No images in the form of thoughts that act as a censor are left to keep your consciousness stuck in rights and wrongs.

When these thoughts become uncontrolled, the negative feelings float around for a prolonged period, we get depressed and finally our whole perspective on life, people and situations changes from that of an opportunity to adversity. Be aware of your inner states consciously to realise the hidden opportunities in any situation or challenge. Spotting opportunities is an act of consciousness. It becomes easy to spot them when we have the ability to see thoughts, not as our enemy, but instead use them wisely till we locate the 'off' button. When one keeps practicing this, which is fairly easy, especially when compared to suffering, one starts to become present and powerful.

Keep Emptying the Contents of the Ego

Just keep noting the ramblings of your ego. You will realise there are some areas for which your mind keeps referring to your past memories and sending suggestions as thoughts to protect you: parents, life partner, friends, work, security, respect in the society, health and appearance are the major areas. In these too the most important area is the "sense of acceptance" from your own people. If you are aware of your area of concerns, you would very easily be able to see the nature of your thoughts. Somewhere when you feel insecure and unloved, the mind craves importance, attention and appreciation from other people. For appreciation you get dependent on situations, business and work. Your entire search for material success stems from the need to have people in your life who love and accept you. But this way you also become scared of losing them. If they are no longer there in your life, the mind feels scared because it has not seen the power of your consciousness.

After a period of time when your reactive behaviour pipes down, when you rarely get disturbed by outside events, what people say and by your own fragmented perceptions, then your ego gets calmer and you become aware.

Don't run after happiness, stay still and you will experience it. It means when the mind is still and free from the ego, when the mind is neither getting attracted by something nor rejecting something, you are in control and so the functional ego ceases to exist.

One has to understand that happiness is our basic state of being and that chasing happiness is an activity triggered by the ego, which actually takes us farther away from happiness.

The problem with the ego is, it understands the value of things only when it loses what it has got. It's like a fish that does not know that it is in the ocean till you take it out, put it on hot sand for a few minutes and put it back in the ocean. Likewise, you don't see what you have got but keep running after what you don't have, thinking that that one missing thing will give you pleasure. So open your inner eyes and see the beautiful life you have. See what you have got; you can see, speak, hear and think for yourself.

**There is no pain in the world. It's the meaning that
we attach to situations that creates the pain.**

If you stop judging and evaluating every situation and every word you hear, there will be no pain. The very evaluation and interpretation causes the pain, as we don't see situations as they are but try to construct them with our shallow experience and knowledge. Evaluation is important but only in moderation and only when it is required, not during every moment we live. Because of over-planning we experience only conditional happiness, which is pleasure. Happiness actually lies in the experiencing and not in jumping with excitement all the time. Consciously changing low mood into high energy is a skill and the biggest tool for creating happiness. Work and live in a way that your family, friends, company and boss need you and not the other way round. In the material world, true happiness comes when others want you and true sadness when you want others. Others want you only when you can contribute something to their lives.

Notice that all the motivating films and WhatsApp messages that you admire are based on people who have been challenged by either life or people and they have come out with flying colours. Who admires Kingfisher scion Vijay Mallya today, considering all the glamour was bought with other people's money? Only phoney people admire phoney money. Real people admire reality and not fantasies of what should be.

See for yourself: what all did you have in terms of possessions like a bank balance, car, house or life partner ten years ago and what you have now, today? You will see that your wealth and possessions have risen manifold and on the contrary, your peace of mind has gone down by manifolds, too.

Why Does the Ego Make Us Suffer?

You are not suffering because you don't have material wealth or respect but because your mind has been made insensitive and incompetent by the ego. You lack the know-how and practical intelligence required to correctly use the mind and to handle challenges. A mind that associates and reacts impulsively is an unintelligent mind. Whereas, a mind that associates memories instantaneously and has the ability to pause and see whether or not a thought is appropriate in the present is an intelligent mind.

The egoistic approach has failed to generate holistic success because we sulk about what might happen because of the past thoughts instead of acting on the now. So till the time we follow the ego's traditional approach, we are living a life dictated by others, that is, simply following what is taught and just earning money and fame without developing an inner vision and a strong mind, which require facing difficult situations.

Consciousness Technique

Are you aware of the consequences of each of your actions, thoughts, intentions and the way your mind perceives things by looking at the results?

Problem in Living with the Existing State of Mind

The very nature of material things, including thoughts, is based on the principle of change. There are few principles of our nature too, like the principle of gravity; whether you are rich or poor, if you fall from the terrace, you will crash to the ground. In the same way, anything that consists of matter, including our bodies, is going to change. Anything derived from external things and situations will change; circumstances, people, time, thoughts, health, wealth and the so-called happiness. So our premise of life and happiness is based on something which is bound to change, is uncertain and absolutely unstable. This makes us afraid, worried and insecure as we know from the depth of our hearts that we cannot be healthy all the time, we cannot produce results all the time, we cannot be promoted all the time, we cannot get respect all the time and we cannot hold on to our relations all the time. The strangest thing is, despite knowing all this, we continue our pursuit of happiness, which makes our minds dull.

9

The Dull Mind

The mind remains dull when it is not developed by its own efforts, own thinking and by facing challenges on its own. It remains dull when it is made from what it has been told what to do or not do by others. When it continuously follows this pattern of asking others for guidance and help, following its past experiences, its thinking becomes mechanical and our responses automatic. When parents scold children for making mistakes, they neither understand what the parents are trying to teach them nor do they learn to try something new and because of the fear of consequences, many remain dull. The problem is, a dull mind that has almost no energy, no matter how hard it tries, looks only at what cannot be done and why things won't work. Moreover, instead of understanding things, we keep trying to change them and our inability to do so make us even less confident.

A dull mind does not know anything new, original or genuine. Howsoever hard you try to think with the existing mind, it will yield only non-satisfactory results. Internally we all know how we feel when we are not handling a situation well. If someone consumes too much alcohol, the problem is not drinking. The problem is an escapist tendency, an uncreative approach and the incapability to face challenges and learn from them. A person who is unable to handle things is basically disturbed from within. It is so important to realise that taking solace in alcohol or in people after a level only makes you dependent. This way the attention that could have been used for handling the challenge is diverted to the problem and the mind suggests running away instead of facing it upfront.

Ego Makes You Weak

You make big goals and plans and don't put in the required efforts, nor do you learn the skills required to achieve them. A mind which has no faith is radar-less and disturbed, and anything done out of a disturbed mind will produce more disturbing results. What people do instead of facing their challenges is ask God, "Why the challenge?" The egoistic mind will always crave help, support and you cannot get the right insight till you experience helplessness. When you become helpless, the thoughts stop because they are the ones telling you that you are helpless. The moment thoughts cease, you are able to clearly see the challenge, and the conserved energy from all the thinking helps in handling the situation as there is now clarity in perception.

> You shouldn't judge a situation and act but rather judge your capacity to handle the situation and respond. Everybody has a way of looking at things. The way you look at things determines the quality of your life.

When you face challenging situations, you get upset and you see life from that perspective. Everything looks upside down, nothing looks set. You see life with a negative attitude, a negative approach and are unable to enjoy what life has to offer. What you already have also disappears from your view. There are no challenges in the present time; situations impact us because we have not dealt with them in the past when they appeared in another form. Your father scolded you and you didn't handle it properly then, so when boss scolds you, you are incapable of dealing with him, too. Had you handled yourself well in the past, you could handle things in the present as well.

A problem-free life doesn't exist.

A weak tree doesn't fall because of the wind; it falls because it is weak. It would have fallen as it is. The wind is just an excuse, a medium. You don't fail because of the situations that surround you, situations are just excuses. You fail because of your weakness and not because of your situations or other people's strength.

Preserving Freshness of the Mind

When your ego feels it has done something good, it goes back to it over and over again to have the pleasure initially experienced. Similarly, when you do something that is wrong as per your mind's standards, it keeps repeating the thoughts of that to avoid the resulting effect in the future. This is its survival mechanism. In both conditions mental energy gets drained. When you act without thinking about the outcome and respond to the situation at hand, you will neither think in terms of pleasure nor pain. This saves energy; you are available, in the present moment, operating from the present and hence experience life in the real sense. When you live while thinking pleasant thoughts or unpleasant thoughts, your energy is wasted.

There are many people who can't observe their thoughts. But it is very important to witness them as your consciousness has to be empty of these worriers. In such a case, one can be aware of what they say, do and behave as all these are generated from thoughts. So even if you can't distance yourself from them, this way you can know the quality of the thought, whether it is negative or positive. If your actions are negative and you feel pathetic then you have the answer. Mere observation leads to detachment from the ego. The very observation is the breaking of identification from the ego. You don't have to dwell on every thought.

Thoughts create illusions and they take the place of perception. Total perception exists where there is no movement of thought. Such a mind uses thoughts only when necessary. What is happening out there is no different from what is happening in here. The root cause of all our problems is our thinking. The only way out of the mind is to understand its functions and not let its functions use consciousness. When you resist there is dissipation of energy. When I decided to become an author there was a lot of resistance from my mind. It took me quite a while to create new pathways in my brain, to sit and write. The transformation from being an extrovert to an introvert could take place only with the help of consciousness. Notice our whole concept of the mind revolves around being accepted, appreciated and acknowledged by our people. When our own people don't appreciate us for who we are, we try to earn money to gain respect. What a pity. What a waste of life. We turn against our own people because according to us they don't respect us, so we work hard to prove them wrong, even though this entire image exists only in our minds. Hence, there is so much violence in our relationships today – father is competing with the son, mother with daughter, brother with sister, husband with wife.

All struggles are a result of the resistance that comes from the ego. When you go through anything completely, you start knowing how far to go, when to exit and how much to accept. The best thing is when you do it with awareness then you don't even need the will to persevere. It comes to you naturally. Then there are no expectations of the ego, so whatever happens is bliss for you. The ego was the one who was resisting. Life was always blissful. There is no possibility of suffering. How can there be? Even tsunamis help reduce suffering in their own way. Such catastrophes make people realise how short life can be, and make them value it. Only when you maintain a positive outlook can you stay connected to your purpose and not lose focus. Always create a good and positive image of the other person in your head. When you do that you go afresh and don't recreate the past over and over again when you meet them.

Life Brings Challenges

It doesn't matter whatever advantages you have – intelligence, money, a great personality, connections or respect in the society. None of these provide a magical wand for an easy existence. How we meet these challenges depends on us and makes a huge difference to whether we end up successful or a failure in life.

The question is, is there any reason for all this misery and suffering or is life absolutely random with its never-ending volley of events that keeps us off balance and barely able to cope? There is. In retrospect, there is a pattern and purpose for everyone. Whenever challenges come your way, they will make you more aware of your inner purpose. It's only during trying times that our hidden skills and intelligence come to the fore which we encash later by putting them to use at work, enhancing our performance. We understand this when we don't just focus on the level of the problem and focus our energy on the "why" of things. There is a larger purpose for all of us and that can only be found by going through challenges. Looking at the "why" of things will make you a victor, while focusing on "why me" will make you a victim. People who depend on others' help can't find the courage to do things on their own. Consider yourself lucky when you don't get help. This is the time when one gets to know his or her hidden skills. You will experience courage only when it is needed otherwise courage does not surface when everything is smooth and sailing. Everything also becomes smooth when there is courage.

Whatever is happening to you is happening because of you and to test what you are going to do.

Developing the ability to see every challenge as the next step to expand your consciousness is what tough times are for. Use every situation to develop yourself. If there is no salt in the food then build a mood that helps you even enjoy bland food but don't complain and waste the opportunity. If salt is available nearby, use it to better the dish otherwise keep enjoying what is there. This way you will learn not to get dependent even on the smaller things. Change what you can, otherwise learn and grow but stay centred, that is, don't leave your consciousness and don't start blaming the situation or people. The moment you notice the negatives in a situation, you become negative yourself. Your consciousness gets coloured and instead of taking charge and doing what is required to be done, you lose energy and focus. Thoughts can be changed when the deeper meaning of things that is hidden in difficult situations is understood. These difficult situations contain the seed for taking charge of your mind and exposing the ego. The moment consciousness takes charge, the birth of intrinsic intelligence happens. Fear cannot exist when intelligence is flowing because fear is a function of the egoistic mind that occurs due to unintelligence.

Intrinsic Intelligence

Intrinsic intelligence surfaces in challenging times. There is a beautiful old Zen story in which a man was a master thief in Japan; he was well known and famous all over the country. And of course, nobody had ever been able to catch hold of him. He was never caught red-handed – although everybody knew that he was the one involved – he had been stealing even from the treasury of the king. And he left his signature on every robbery, so everybody knew who had been there. In fact, it had become fashionable to brag about being targeted by him, because the master thief had thought you were worthy of stealing something from. People would brag, saying, "Last night the master came to our house." But the thief was getting older and one day his young son said to him, "Now you are getting old, teach me your art." The father said, "I was also thinking about the same, but unfortunately it is not an art but a knack. I cannot teach it to you as it cannot be taught, only caught." That's what being successful is like, it cannot be taught, it has to be caught. That's the difference between a teacher and a master. The teacher teaches, the master makes himself available to be caught, to be learnt from. You have to imbibe his spirit. If you only listen to his words you will miss his meaning. You can only learn if you start catching the spirit behind his words. That's why listening is so important. So the thief said to his son, "Then come with me tonight, because this is not something that can be taught. You can only imbibe the spirit of me; if you are intelligent enough, you will catch it. I cannot give it to you, but you will get it."

Naturally, the son was afraid as the wall of the palace was broken in front of him the first time. Even in old age the father's hands were like a surgeon's – unwavering, unshaking and fearless, as if he was breaking the wall of his own home. He was so certain of his art he did not even look around to check if someone was watching them. And his young son was trembling; it was a cold winter night and yet the son was perspiring. The father was doing everything silently. Then the father entered the palace. The son followed, his knees trembling; he was worried that he might fall any moment. He was losing all consciousness because of his fear. What if they were caught? The father was moving in the dark as if it was his house, he knew everything about it, and he could move without stumbling against the furniture even in the dark, making no noise at all. Noiselessly he reached into the innermost chamber of the palace.

He opened a cupboard and told the son to reach in and find the valuables. As soon as the son entered it, the father locked the door shouting, "Thief! A thief! Wake up!" and escaped through the hole they had dug in the wall. The son could not understand, now he was locked in the cupboard, trembling, perspiring and the whole palace was awake. People were searching for the thief. *What kind of father is this? He has ensured my death, and what kind of teaching is this?* He thought. He had never even imagined something of this sort happening. His father had created a living nightmare for him. Now he will certainly be caught. He was really very angry – anyone would be in his situation – but there was no point in being angry. Something had to be done that very moment and he couldn't think of anything. His mind had simply stopped working.

The mind cannot figure out what it is all about, what to do, because all that it knows is useless; it has never been in such a situation before. And the mind can move only in the world already known to it. Whenever anything unknown is encountered, the mind stops. It is a machine. If you have not fed it with the right information before, it cannot work, it cannot function. Now this was such a new situation, the young man could not conceive a way out. There was nothing to do. After one hour when the son finally reached home, the father was fast asleep, snoring. He threw aside his blanket and said, "What nonsense is this?" The father said, "So you are back. No need to tell me the whole story – you also go to sleep. Now you know the art and we need not discuss it." But the son said, "I have to tell you the whole story, what happened."

The father said, "You can if you want to, otherwise, I don't need to hear it. That you have returned is enough proof. Now from tomorrow, you are on your own. You have got the innate intelligence and awareness that a thief needs. I am immensely happy with you." But the son couldn't contain his eagerness, he wanted to relate the whole thing – he had done such a great job. He said, "Just listen, otherwise I will not be able to sleep at all. I am so excited. You almost killed me."

The father said, "It was hard, but that's how a master has to act many times. Tell me the whole story, what happened?"

He said, "Out of nowhere – not from any intellect, and certainly not from my mind this has happened."

The father said, "This is the key to self-mastery that enables mastering all the fields of life, whether you are a thief or a professional, whether you are a lover or a scientist, a painter or a poet, it doesn't matter. Whatsoever the field may be, this is the master key – nothing happens from the head, everything happens from somewhere else. Call it consciousness, call it intuition, call it mindlessness, call it meditation – these are different names for the same thing. It has started functioning. I can see it on your face; I can see the aura around you. You are going to become a fine thief, and remember that this mastery over theft has been my path to attaining meditation.

The son said, "When I was standing inside that damned cupboard and people were searching for the thief, a servant came with a candle in her hand, I could see through the keyhole. From nowhere, out of spontaneity, out of intuition, I started making noises, like I was a cat – and I have never done it before. The servant, thinking that there was a cat in the cupboard, unlocked it. As she unlocked it – I don't know how I did it – it happened! I blew the candle out, pushed the woman away, and ran. People followed me – almost a dozen people were following me carrying torches and lamps, they were coming closer and closer and I was on the verge of being caught.

Then suddenly I came across a well. I saw a rock just beside the well. I didn't believe that I had the strength to lift that rock, but it happened. I took the rock and threw it in the well and then stood by the side of the tree to watch what happened. It was all happening, I was not doing it. People surrounded the well. They thought the thief had jumped into the well and died. They all went back."

The father said, "Now I can die happily because I know I am leaving somebody who knows the art. This is how my father, your grandfather taught me. One has to takes risks to learn, to develop reasoning, intelligence and skill to ensure success. Mentors don't make champions, opponents do. Learn to handle yourself when scared rather than expecting easy situations. Anything that you approach with a relaxed and blissful energy won't scare you because it isn't the adversary that scares you, you scare yourself."

Keep working to get the solution rather than hovering above the problem. Looking at problems will deaden you. Looking for solutions will enliven you.

Mahatma Gandhi was a very staunch believer of non-violence. Once it so happened that a calf got cancer in his Ashram and was in deep pain. Gandhiji requested that the doctors give poison to the calf. Now, people in the Ashram and those who were staying nearby got very irritated saying, "You are the one who says that one should be non-violent and killing of a calf is sin, how could you have asked the doctors to poison the calf then?" Gandhiji said, "I cannot see the calf in such pain and I have confirmed with the doctor that the cancer is not curable."

People who do not use their intelligence and only go by the book, principles and laws will always have trouble understanding life and that's why they keep complaining. Life requires a very different kind of intelligence. This is practical intelligence that starts to develop when one becomes aware and escapes the ego, experiencing everything by one's own intelligence rather than constantly justifying his acts or searching for what he read in books.

Block out all the old voices telling you what is right and what is wrong and never fear condemnation from people. When I started my training company, everybody was against me including my family and friends. But somewhere deep down I knew this is it for me. We carry the past as we are scared to experiment with the new. You "fast" without experiencing what your body is feeling because that's what the traditions say. There are people in India who give gifts to their relatives beyond their means just to get respect from others. One has to be realistic rather than being positive and negative about things. Operate from your understanding and intelligence to keep the complaining away and experience inner growth. And when you don't, you keep developing and strengthening what you already know, the past. There is no room for the new.

Get in touch with your inner child. If you ever watch small children, you will notice just how free they are and how little they care about what other people think of them. They are happy and live in the moment. They reflect their true natures and intelligence. They have not yet been conditioned to "fit in" to a society that squashes their inner self. They don't care if people think that they are silly while they dance in the front yard for all the neighbours to see. Children are just pure love and light. If you really want to get in touch with your inner intelligence, become free. Play, have fun, enjoy the moment, do cartwheels in the front yard. Realise how stiff and serious we have become. We play roles to fit into society and we suppress our true nature out of fear of what others think. If you find yourself worrying about being judged, remember that is just the conditioned you, not the real you.

Sometimes Burning Yourself is Good

If I tell you, "Look, that is fire, don't go near it or else you will burn yourself," you will listen to me and safeguard yourself by not going near the fire. Till here it is all good. But imagine you are in your bedroom and your house is on fire. Since you have never burnt yourself in the past, you might take it lightly and say, "It's all right, there may be some fire but I will handle it later. right now let me sleep." What will happen? You will burn to death. If you get this, you will get the importance of learning only from your own experience.

The intrinsic intelligence, the energy inside will see that you get what is required for your survival. Resources for your existence too are assured till the time nature wants you to live. So there is no fear. Fear arises from your insecurity about tomorrow and you keep getting support when you don't doubt tomorrow.

Once I had a massive financial crunch and I had to ask a friend to return the two lakh rupees that I had invested with him. Due to certain reasons and market conditions, it got delayed. I said to myself that I don't want to take a loan and didn't fear the future at all. Since the money was there with my friends, there was no need to worry. Something inside me told me that I want to try just going with whatever happens, I wanted to see whether the clues I am getting from my intuition work or not. After a few days, I received my refund of some Rs. 3.5 lakh from the Income Tax Department. Earlier I believed in fate but now I knew nature through my own experience instead of following it blindly. This does not discard the need for hard work or planning in advance but when you work hard and trust fate, you keep getting lucky.

Ego Wants Help

The moment you expect help, the inner energy of the consciousness disappears, as now there is no need for it; you have already got the support from outside. All outside support will make you handicapped, dependent and dull. Keep rejecting help but if people need your help and support, be there for them and do whatever you can for them. You will understand this when you start practicing it, you will understand everything when you start living it.

Krishna's Consciousness

Once Lord Krishna was having lunch, and his wife, Rukmani, was serving. All of a sudden he got up and rushed outside the house. Rukmani was surprised and she asked, "Lord, what happened? Why have you left midway?" Without saying a word, he left the house. But he returned just after few minutes. Rukmani, puzzled, asked him, "What happened? You have never done this before." Krishna said, "I divined that some people were throwing stones at a man who loves me, who was chanting my name, so I went to save him." Rukmani asked, "So why didn't you save him?" Krishna replied, "Because when I reached there to save him, he too had lifted stones, so now he has made arrangements to protect himself."

Here Lord Krishna represents our consciousness, which is there to help us, and stones represent the ego that works as per its conditionings. In this story the point to be understood is that when you avoid being reactive and hurting others in order to protect yourself, your innate intelligence works and you are free.

A story is a pearl concealed in the onion. What looks certain may not be real. The truth can be completely different. A story is a way of communicating lessons of incredible significance. But one needs to analyse it thoroughly to understand the crux of the message. A story is both effortless and difficult as it is a story on the exterior and a secret within.

So let's look at two stories we have discussed how intellectual knowledge keeps us caged and how wisdom assimilates all the knowledge together and helps us deal with things. Earlier, we spoke about the priest who drowned because of his inaction due to a wrong belief that God will come to protect him. He was lacking practical intelligence. In this second story of Krishna, we are talking about knowing the consciousness with its innate intelligence; it suggests handling situations in a positive way as the ego always makes one reactive and suggests negative ways that eventually harm everybody. This is not to be seen in a context where terrorists are attacking or your sister is threatened by goons but in our day-to-day situations dealing with colleagues at work, family and friends.

Stability of the mind is possible only when we make the mind work and not dance to the ego's tune.

Unlucky People Don't Have Challenges

There are some very unlucky people out there who avoid facing challenges due to the privileges of money and social status and just go through life in a very shallow, superficial way. Life is beautiful when you can see its purpose; some skill, maybe an action plan that unfolds while going through the challenges makes you feel like an architect. You can see the blueprint very clearly and then all your encounters and actions look like they are taking you towards your destination in harmony.

The purpose is to free yourself from your ego and not to keep finding external reasons, like blaming other people, for your failures. If you know where you are going, it won't matter what kind of *dhabhas* or restaurants you get on the way.

When I was failing in my business, the instinct to take risks came to the fore, which I am using now in life to deal with my conditioned mind.

I remember the times I got frustrated writing this book as I didn't come from the relevant background. At a party I attended, I said something very important and everybody ignored it as if they didn't hear me. I vowed to myself, "I will show them what I am and now the whole world will know what I want to say through the book." Though this kind of energy is negative, sometimes it can be converted to positive. The impetus was back. I just kept one thing in mind – I have to learn continuously and respect people as they are. Now I have found calmness so I know that anything that disturbs me is in me and not in them.

One of the biggest and most impactful lessons I learned was from a simple line my cousin brother, Gattu*da*, said, "There should always be free flow of positive emotions, respect for people with humility and absence of arrogance." It just struck me that this is what is missing in me. Despite our intelligence we don't get support from the environment as when we are hurt we talk in a very shrill voice and the ego is felt by others. The universe is always talking to us but we don't listen, we are interested in talking rather than listening. Take your power back from the ego by not giving in to its expectations. Getting hurt is also important as it exposes the ego. Our inner purpose in life is to experience consciousness and use the ego as a stepping stone to removing it. My unease and restlessness settled as I found my purpose in life. The ego leaves you once you let go of it. The ego leaves you once you realise who you are and remain attentive. Attention is fire, it burns the ego and lets you stay rooted in consciousness.

Once a bank paid me Rs. 15,000 extra by mistake. I returned the money on my own without the bank asking for it as they didn't know that they had given me more money than I had withdrawn. I felt as if I should tell everybody that I did such a good deed. My ego wanted to tell the whole world, my friends, family and everybody else. And while just having these thoughts, my attention went on the fact that I started getting disturbed whereas my purpose is to stay peaceful come what may. I told myself, *I want peace and not appreciation from others at the cost of my inner calm.* I kept quiet, didn't tell anyone and felt quietude. For me, running to people for credits and appreciation ceased completely as I have discovered it for myself that this is the biggest reason for stress. Practicing nonchalance started giving me results in the due course of time. When one is aware of the ego, it stops. This makes you centred and a lot of energy is generated and then you don't need any validation from external sources. When you need appreciation, it is because you lack something within and it also makes you avoid challenges.

I kept observing that I was being ignored by people and was made to go through a tough life under nature's grand scheme of things so that I could meet destiny. Destiny not in context of what the astrologer says but the path that is destined for me, for my consciousness, for my soul. Tough times kept on breaking my ego and my original being and nature kept on emerging. I went from being a complicated, confident, street-smart, egoistic, sweet, aggressive, straight-talking, honest, proving, ostentatious nice guy to a compassionate, loving and innately intelligent person – not in comparison to anyone but in the way I now handle my life and my mind.

Critical incidents that helped me wake up were my ailments, my diseases. As mentioned, I got thyroid and that shattered me. It told me that I stay stressed but I still was unable to handle myself till I got tinnitus. This made me realise that I can die anytime, so why live a stressful life? To get to the effortless state, initially I had to put in a lot of effort in observing my mind till it became natural.

Nature gives you clues and if you are committed, you get help.

Whenever my spirits went down, a profound message used to come from either a movie's dialogue or from conversations with my friends or parents. Meeting a few intellectuals also helped. To catch these messages you have to be present to your purpose in life, which is to get out of the robotic state you are in. I used the tinnitus's continuous ticking in my ears as an alarm given to me by nature to check whether I am thinking egotistically or not. The adversity became the biggest gift of nature to be aware all the time. If you have the attention separate from any situation, the situation cannot impact you. Instead of working on the tinnitus, I started working on my attention by keeping away from thinking about it. I got the power to be able to do so from one of the incidents below.

There was a businessman who developed a tumour in his stomach and he asked the doctors to operate on him without anaesthesia. He told the doctors, "I am not going to lose my consciousness at any cost. I have got it after much hard work. Even if I die because of the tumour, it's all right, but now at this stage taking anything that makes me unconscious is unacceptable." The doctors obviously refused his request. He asked the doctors again to test-operate his finger without the anaesthesia saying that when he reads the *Gita* he is absent to the whole world as he is only present to the scripture. The doctors finally did as they were asked and the businessman kept on reading the *Gita* without a sign of the impact of the scalpel on his finger. The doctors were convinced and they operated upon his stomach too to remove the tumour without the anaesthesia. The businessman went into the operation theatre and started reading the *Gita*. The doctors operated on him without the anaesthesia. This was an operation of one of its kind as the businessman could have died if his attention wavered. But the operation was successful. This is the power of the consciousness or pure attention and when it is there the ego is absent.

Material World and the World of Consciousness

When compulsive desires stemming from the mind to achieve your material goals come to an end, and you continue to intentionally do your best, you achieve consciousness. This power will get you out of the rat race and you will win because there is no losing in the world of consciousness. You can lose only if you are operating from the mindset of proving yourself; when the past wins over the present. But when you enjoy everything, even your failures, and keep doing your best, continuously improving yourself, you grow.

It is the mind and expectations that fail, not performances. Every situation is not a problem to be solved but a challenge to be experienced. When you experience it deeply, solutions will flow. This flow will be from that peaceful point inside where your intrinsic intelligence lies. Any action that arises from that intelligence is the right action. So the moment you catch yourself saying, "That's the way I am", it is actually the way your mind is and not you, not your consciousness. People have complaints about not having enough money but never have the same about work. They don't want to work more but want more money. You can experience consciousness when you take up a goal consciously that your limiting beliefs have been stopping you to do and make it happen.

Consciousness Technique

Choose any one thing and make it happen; it can be a new job, learning a language, a new role in the same company, losing weight, working on your anger, developing patience, always saying the truth, being supportive, being in the present or anything that you like.

Material things were meant for giving us more workability so that we could put some more efforts in creating consciousness and experience this beautiful life by expressing what we feel, being innovative in doing things in different ways, connecting with people, meditating while working, being joyful, growing from inside and uplifting mankind. Today, the whole meaning of work has changed. The medium (that is the material desires) to reach the goal of consciousness has become the goal.

The Real Goal

The real goal is being at peace all the time and not just earning money to be happy. It means actions done in a non-attached way, without any expectation of the fruits of labour, all actions done without being motivated by desire. I met an executive in one of my training programs. He was very sad as he got a 30 per cent salary hike whereas he was expecting 50 per cent. Out of stress, he developed diabetes and became extremely cross with people because his expectation failed by 20 per cent. He couldn't see the 30 per cent he got because of the frustration. Such a mind crammed with desires always feels that it is losing, no matter how much it gains. This is what the blind mind does; it always keeps you running as its desires rarely get fulfilled. Such a being is never content irrespective of how successful he becomes as there is no end to expectations.

Material success may follow if you keep doing the right thing. This way whether you get successful in terms of the world or not doesn't matter as you will have inner power and peace and you then are successful as far as living is concerned. Around peace, ego disappears. Pleasure is something temporary that you get from things like partying, alcohol, promotions, appreciation, etc., but the very state of your being where there is no condemnation, criticism or comparison comes with peace and is the real happiness.

> If you work from the material domain, you will be stuck in the competitive domain and remain a slave to other people, always trying to impress them. Even if they get impressed, you still remain a slave as you then are dependent on them forever.

You work hard but sadly with the intention of proving yourself and not to express yourself or explore your hidden talents, which is where all the fun lies and that's what you are paid for. That's the reason people don't have high energy. A majority come to work tired and go back dead. They are not motivated enough to do anything. For them, earning money and respect always come from making others lose. This kind of thought process is not powerful enough to make one put his heart into things; he can only put his mind to things.

Nothing Fails Like Success

You rarely see people who keep achieving things throughout their life. The majority of them have one or two victories in life and then they are stuck. They keep waiting for another achievement, doing the same thing over and over again that got them their first win. I come across many people who say, "We want to work more, put in efforts and achieve the goals that we have set." The problem is the ego's tendency to avoid work, do less work or do whatever it feels is right. The ego gauges what it will get and accordingly lets you perform. It evaluates the potential reward according to its own limited perception and reduces the energy if it doesn't like what it sees.

When You Are Conscious, the Universe Needs You

I noticed when I was busy reacting to situations and people, I started getting less work. The insight I got was that I wasn't healthy enough to do more work and hence companies didn't call me. If they had called me, I would have lost a lot of future business. Thank God, I failed and got less work. I wasn't ready to take up big opportunities mentally, emotionally or physically. When I became present, work attracted me and the companies sought me out, too.

Stumbling Blocks to Stepping Stones

My brother committed suicide and I almost wanted to follow him. I experienced similar anxiety because of the way my ego was making me feel about every unfulfilled expectation. Many a times I had suicidal thoughts but instead I channelised my anxious energy into saving people who go through the same. People who don't want challenges actually live a very challenged life! Going through challenges requires intelligence, kindness and courage. The secret to a powerful life is not success or appreciation but going through life, going through eventualities with calmness and enjoying every second of life by being grateful that you at least have the opportunity to live.

Accepting *what is* gives you a feeling of pride and generates enthusiasm. Your body responds well to the enthusiasm when it feels that spark inside you that indicates that you can do anything. Every moment in life we meet with a challenge, and those who do not accept these challenges die while they are still living. We can see these dead people roaming everywhere. They are only alive physically and will be buried later. So wherever life leads you, go. If life leads you to a fight, then fight. But you should have the wisdom to distinguish between the fights arising from your ego and those coming naturally like the ones that came in Arjuna's life in the *Mahabharata*. Here, fight does not mean a physical fight but refers to putting in efforts for achieving the purpose of your life.

Handling Problems

Say to yourself: no problem is big enough, no problem is serious enough. The mind makes any problem appear big or small as it compares each one with its old memories. If you portray the problem as a big one to the mind, it will deem it so and react accordingly. The very instant you say to yourself that no problem is serious enough, the problem is almost 99 per cent finished. Your whole outlook on it changes. The mind starts supporting this new command received from you, the consciousness. When you handle yourself powerfully, space opens up. If you have a problem, know that it is because of a desire.

If you handle the thought that is responsible for creating the whirlpool of thoughts pondering over whether your desire will be fulfilled or not then you have found the switch. The problem is always the thought and not the desire. If the thoughts cease we will have the energy to actually work on the desire rather than cribbing. Try it now, say to your mind, "I am feeling great and full of energy" and just maintain this for five to ten minutes. You will notice that if you have any pain in your body, it will start vanishing as a majority of pain is psychosomatic and your positive energy and enthusiasm enhance the immune system.

The problem itself is never the problem; it is the thoughts about the problem, which are the problem. Detaching yourself from these thoughts is the key to solving all your problems. If you are an aggressive person, you think that you are angry most of the time and then you are indulging your anger. That is where things are going wrong. Getting carried away *Justifying keeps you there, caged in the mind.* with the anger means supporting the very thought of anger with your unconsciousness and furthering the problem by thinking about it. This adds fuel to anger. The moment you pay attention to it, there is a disconnection from the mind and its criticizing mode. Choose what you want, wallowing in hurt or creating something. Instead of trying to remove anger, being peaceful will work better.

Access to a Sharp Mind

Anything that annoys you also teaches you patience. Anyone who abandons you teaches you how to stand on your own feet. Anything that angers you teaches you forgiveness and compassion. Anything that has power over you teaches you to take your power back. Anything you hate teaches you unconditional love. Anything you fear teaches you how to overcome your fear. Anything you can't control teaches you how to let go. To be healthy and hearty, one needs to accept the nature of one's mind completely. Only through acceptance of one's nature can the door to reality be found. The nature of our mind is the door to our existence.

Just accept that your mind is the way it is. This very acceptance is an act of consciousness and you are pulled out of the ego's whirlpool. But if you get into judgments and evaluations as to who is right and who is wrong and continue justifying yourself and proving others as the culprits or vice versa then you will fall into the ego game. Justifying keeps you there, caged in the mind. If you can see this, you will act. Consciousness gives you a vision to act on and from that vision a discipline emerges from the inside. This way you don't act out of compulsion, you just act out of choice and insight. You will stay in the office till late hours if required, not to prove something to the boss, but because you will see the urgency. Rewards then are not money or a promotion but an inner satisfaction that you did the right thing. Success can't help but follow.

Majority of us go through life inattentively, reacting only to the surroundings in which we are living. These reactions create further bondage. When you give total attention, consciously, to these conditionings of your mind, you realise that there is no problem as big as your own mind and the ego. All problems are created by your own mind expecting things. When the mind doesn't get a perfect husband for you as per your expectations after reading a trunkful of *Mills & Boons*, it reacts and you become sad.

When you are present, you accept reality as it is and create results out of it. You stop expecting things and situations that are not there and work to get them. There is a difference between the two, one will keep you waiting and the other will take you towards what you want.

When you are conscious, the mishaps that happen to you will not impact you.

Consciousness operates from reality and it knows that anything can happen anytime. This knowledge helps use the mind in such situations and an intuitive self also emerges to our rescue. If thoughts come and you are able to pause before reacting instantaneously then you are responding. But if the consciousness flows away in the current, then you lose it. The content of the consciousness is its thoughts, intentions, relationships, desires, fear, insecurities and sorrows as it connects with the mind. If you become completely aware of your current field of consciousness then you will have the secret tool – **attention**.

Here we are talking about the energy of attention. See what's there in your consciousness right now: anger, fear, jealousy, hatred, disgust, depression, insecurity, anxiety or joy. Give it all your attention. Don't do anything. Don't flow with any of the emotion that's there. With full attention – that is with your eyes, ears and nerves – observe them. The very moment you are able to see these feelings and thoughts, a disconnect takes place. When the energy of the consciousness is not attached to these feelings, you feel light and relaxed as the energy that was earlier getting dissipated in anger and other emotions is available to you now. This is attention. When you look at the content of your consciousness, that is the thoughts, intentions and desires completely and with total awareness, you get to attention.

Concentration is exclusion. When you concentrate, you focus only on one thing, whereas attention includes everything. It encompasses what you are reading right now, the maid cleaning the house, the sound of the air-conditioner, your wife watching TV and with all the senses active, you are aware of the inner feelings, intentions and on top of it you are also attentive to what you are reading. If you are concentrating, then any form of interference by your wife will disturb you, because you are concentrating on one thought only: reading. Attention is inclusive and only then can it furnish a holistic approach of looking at things. But the problem is that most of us are not aware of either inward or outward things. So if you want to understand what your boss is trying to say, you would have to give it your whole attention, which is consciousness by first knowing yourself. Ego resists the present moment. Working from the mind comes from inside the mind. But training the mind comes from the consciousness. The mind is a vessel that collects information through senses and reacts according to the past memories. Wisdom lies in not letting the collected information get impacted by the past and using it consciously in the present circumstances when the action is done. Wisdom by default gives birth to action.

Wisdom is Action and Ego is Reaction

If the ego only reacts then who is taking decisions on our behalf? The past conditioning, concepts, labels, judgments, images, words, assumptions, desires and definitions are the sources of our decisions. Take a moment to think: have I ever done conscious thinking on my own? The meaning of thinking on your own is seeing things the way they are, without interpreting them from the mind, based on past data. On your own you will be vibrant, otherwise you will remain dull as the mind always sees others and compares. Then only you can know what the ability to think on your own is. Your thoughts are not your thoughts, you have gathered them.

The process: throw all thoughts that are not yours out of the window. Avoid thinking other people's thoughts, be original. Now, also see where you think from – fear or love. All thoughts that come from fear are not yours; you lie about something, you manipulate circumstance, you misguide someone, you misrepresent yourself. Notice carefully all that you say to others. Is it just to save the situation, prove yourself right or do you speak your truth?

Who is it that you try saving all the time? What is in you that protects itself even at the cost of destroying you? Can you say how things are irrespective of it being right or wrong? Do you really want to get out of the suffering? Ask yourself. If yes, then this is the process that will develop you from within, make you a man and make you mature, too. Dodging people is akin to dodging yourself. Don't dodge, be authentic. Speak only that, which you have known through your experience. Don't keep a religious fast or go to the temple because people have told you to do so. Experience things for yourself and see what happens and what thoughts you have. Do you feel uncomfortable? If you have experienced discomfort in fasting, trust me, it won't get you closer to God. But if you do any one thing on your own accord, then you become the god of your universe and then you can be creative in the right sense.

How do you know which thought is yours and which thought is a borrowed one? If a thought has potential and has power, then it is your thought. If you feel under confident then you are trying to be someone else that you are not.

Keep finding your consciousness in this ocean of thoughts, values and beliefs.

So why is it important to have your own thoughts? It is important because if what you think and understand is not right, the outcome of your whole life is bound to be wrong. All your actions are dependent on your understanding of events and situations and if your understanding is not yours and is based on other people's thoughts and ideas, your whole life will be a second-hand one. If the understanding is right, then all seeds and your originality should bloom into what they are supposed to be. Whatever is hidden within will blossom.

The first step towards having a successful life is to realise, through your sufferings, that what you are doing and the direction in which you are moving are completely wrong and no about-turn will be possible if you don't stop. If you are enjoying the struggle and deep down you know that whatever you are doing will yield results, then you are on the right path. And if you are suffering whatever you are doing is wrong.

So ask yourself – how am I living? Whatever I am doing, will it have a substantial outcome? Will I gain anything out of this? Will I reach anywhere? Will it actually put an end to my running? Will I ever be at peace or continue suffering because of my emotions?

10

The World of Emotions

Emotions are like alcohol. They take over your reasoning, make you drunk. The problem is that they are as false as the ego, they are based on what we have been told and not on our own findings. Your emotions are not actually yours. When the ego faces something that it doesn't like, negative emotions are produced. Unfelt or suppressed, negative emotions like anger, resentment and guilt are dense sensations and block our energy.

The mind needs convincing answers. Any eventuality, if understood well, doesn't give the mind any scope for disturbances. If the situation is not understood or faced fully, the emotions produced will be frozen. These frozen emotions stick and remain as traces for future insecurity, fear, aggression, rage, mood swings and disease. The fact is, everybody goes through emotional pain in their childhood. The story starts even before birth, we have all heard stories of infants being conscious in the womb. When a child is in the womb, he is totally secure with an in-room dining service and has everything that he could possibly want without having to move one bit. When he comes out he is pampered and loved, of course, though some don't get that. However, when the child grows up and joins this unconscious world, all his expectations start shattering.

He has to provide for himself with everything, clothing, housing, food, career, respect, a partner and friends, everything has to be earned. And as we all know, it is not easy. When the expectations start breaking on unpleasant conditions, right from childhood, it turns into an energy field. It then reflects in your personality, blocking the flow of your natural emotions completely.

Emotional blocks are built on unfulfilled expectations. Does that mean if your expectations are met, you won't have such blocks? No. In the first place, no one's expectations can be fulfilled as they are not real but rather made out of illusions and the conditioning we get from other people. Secondly if considering a hypothetical condition where all expectations are fulfilled, blocks will still keep developing as expectations come from the past and life is happening in the present always throwing new situations at us.

Emotional Blocks

Emotional blockages are created by negative experiences, unresolved emotional wounds, self-destructive behaviour, patterns and self-limiting beliefs. Emotional blocks counter intentions contributing to self-sabotage. They act as a defence mechanism to deal with deep emotional pain experienced in traumatic and destructive situations ranging from the loss of a loved one, betrayal, and abuse to rejection, and so on. But instead of dealing with eventualities, they make us scared and fearful.

Once the emotional disturbances are not there you can move on and handle other things. Personally, I had developed a massive emotional block against my friends and family members. This is when I was going through a tough phase in life (which I now understand was important for me). I started expecting my friends and family to support me. They supported me, but when you are low and down, you don't see what you are getting and focus only on what you are expecting. I felt that nobody even bothered asking me what I was going through. I started wondering whether it was that people were really insensitive, or it was because of my own ego, or people themselves were stuck in their world dealing with their issues. Deep down I was expecting compassion, which I now realise, is possible only when one is present and not just blindly running after pleasure, and not just helping those who will help in the future or are influential, which means helping is an act of your own love and care, with no ulterior motives. Not because you will get something in return but because you have gotten so much that you want to give something back. This indicates that your consciousness is empty of its content completely and thus there are no blocks.

I felt my expectations were genuine as I was not looking for money from anyone but just a few healing words. But what broken expectations taught me could not have been possible had I got few consoling words.

When a person does not operate from his own wisdom, he keeps looking at how other people behave with him and feels as if he has to keep facing the blasts, rejection, wrath and anger of other people. He feels he will be complete only when his expectations and desires are fulfilled. And when his expectations shatter, he also breaks. To expect is to escape. Blocks become judgments; I will/won't do this, he did this... If one keeps an open mind and an accepting attitude, blocks don't form in his mind.

One of the major reasons for going down and having low energy is your habit of beating yourself up, feeling guilty, inappropriate, unwanted and rejected. It's important to see and experience when one has not acted out of his own code of conduct or as per the agreed conduct of the society. This is the only way where one can correct, learn and develop the self.

**Only the irritated irritate and the already irritated
get more irritated.**

Ego leads to guilt or hubris and both are dangerous for us as one makes us feel low about ourselves and the other makes us arrogant and high. This causes trouble in the conscious calm energy of our being, in relationships, in emotions and the body. This makes us highly reactive.

Notice, many go through a sudden emotional reaction while having a normal conversation, say, with their partner. Has this ever happened to you? The conversation goes from mundane to a hot volcanic explosion and at times it's like a cold wave when one person shuts down and becomes completely indifferent. See in retrospect, perhaps you were talking about routine work to be done or paying the electricity bill. It can also happen during a simple discussion about an upcoming wedding in the family or chatting about some another person. You are taken by surprise as without an explanation, your other half either starts shouting, yelling and blaming you or might even suddenly withdraw.

Impact of Positive and Negative Emotions

We experience a range of emotions. From joy to depression and happiness to sadness, they all make us feel different things within our bodies. Our brain produces serotonin, dopamine or oxytocin when we feel happy and releases cortisol when we are stressed. These hormones create a different environment in the body and colour our perception. When stressed, we remain in survival mode and look at things negatively. When happy, our level of acceptance and tolerance rises.

Imagine what will happen when you think negative thoughts

all the time. The brain being a very powerful tool, starts moulding our actions according to what we define our thoughts as, what something is or should be. Our awareness increases in that particular direction and we start seeing those clues easily.

So when we are in the negative state of mind, we see only what is wrong. For example, when you are driving and someone cuts you off, you may lose your temper, altering your mood. On the other hand, there may be many people who, when they get cut off, simply apply the brakes and move on with their day as if nothing happened. In this case, the same experience is felt differently by different people. One sees it as negative while the other doesn't. We have all experienced these different states and moods where sometimes nothing touches us and at times we are just waiting for a trigger to reveal our already impacted state. That simply means that things are neither positive nor negative. It's we who define things as positive and negative. There are in fact no positive or negative experiences other than what the mind defines as such. All the power lies within us, in our very perception of an experience or situation. This gives us immense freedom to move beyond our definitions of each experience and move into consciousness where we simply accept each experience for what it is instead of condemning or imagining what could have been.

Negative Energy and Drama Pattern

Whenever we face a negative situation in life, the existing blocks get activated and further get fortified because of the new ones. If you notice, there is a dramatic pattern in many of us that vividly gets demonstrated in our relationships. The emotional blocks are one of the factors that keep us sad, unhappy and full of sorrow. These blocks thrive on ego-driven activities and become habits, keeping us entangled almost all the time in picking up petty issues. We start majoring in minor things. Since we are blind to our own selves, we point out these blocks in others very easily. We notice how our mother reacts, how our friends talk in a sharp tone or even the way the boss talks so aggressively and the way our partner behaves indifferently at times. But seeing all this we miss that all these people are actually reacting to our own emotional blocks. This is the best way to self-awareness, if you are able to see the cause of people's behaviour in your own self rather than trying to correct them.

These blocks are rarely dormant and it's very easy to find unconscious people everywhere, triggering our unconsciousness by catching on to what people say and do. And many a times we activate this blocked energy by interpreting a positive event as a negative one. Even when we are alone, our egoistic nature plays a big role in keeping these blocks alive by persistently thinking negative thoughts. The problem is when these emotional blocks get activated, they hijack thinking completely, making our personality negatively drunk in emotional energy and the people around experience our vibes and find us obnoxious.

If you notice, the ego then keeps repeating those incidents that made you sad or unhappy in the form of thoughts about yourself, others, the past and future. When you are not conscious, you get identified with these stories, taking them as words from God and something that you are meant to suffer. It's very crucial to break this habit before it gets really hardwired and becomes a permanent part of people's personalities. Once it gets permanent, you start feeling them as a part of *you* and take it for granted that this is the way you are. Then you very frequently start feeling emotionally drained as negative thoughts coupled with emotional blocks consume your energy completely, leaving you listless.

How Emotional Blocks Manifest in Life

The emotional body is magnetic and holds on to suppressed emotions until you allow them to move, by expressing them. Unreleased emotions hinder human beings from raising bodily vibes and frequencies and can result in physical manifestations like chronic pain, anxiety, migraines, ulcers, and other forms of illness.

Ego is so preoccupied that it stays oblivious to the connection between your mind and body. The connection is very powerful and since it cannot be visually seen, the ego misses the effects your mind can have on your physical body which are intense. We can learn to be conscious with awareness and have an overall positive mental attitude to deal with our internal challenges directly and in turn create a healthy lifestyle. Since the ego is unaware of its own negativity and self-destructive thoughts, instead of dealing with our internal issues, it covers those issues with positive self-talk, shunning the issues, by not paying them any attention or finding a way out. Negative emotions disturb harmony in the field of consciousness and can be very easily observed when one feels anxiety, fear, anger, sorrow, hatred, jealousy and envy paving the way for unease and "dis-ease" in the body, lowering the body's natural resistance system. If you ask doctors today, you would know that majority of the diseases such as diabetes, thyroid, hypertension, skin allergies and many other in people who are volatile and hyper-sensitive are caused by these damaging emotions.

Emotional Memory

Our emotions and experiences are essentially energy which gets stored in the cellular memory of our bodies. I have experienced that when something in our life happens, it leaves a memory or pain in a certain area of our body. In that particular area of the body, you keep feeling as if something is still happening. It seems we still hold energy released from that experience which hasn't escaped our body. If you observe sharply, when you have a disease or a pain, stiffness, or injuries in certain areas, it's often related to something that you are emotionally feeling. It remains unnoticed initially as we are stuck in our thoughts and are not fully present to our feelings.

Injuries and Blocked Emotions

I am reminded of an incident; I was going through a tough time in a relationship and my own willingness to continue the relationship was missing. Often, it so happens that your ego makes you do certain things out of emotions and your consciousness does not get aligned with these acts. One such time I had an ankle injury that turned a small sprain into my worst nightmare. I was on my morning jog and sprained my ankle. Being an athlete, I used to turn the ankle during such sprains making it harder to settle the muscle. But this time it worked adversely and a massive pain developed in my ankle joint. I spent hours with masseurs and at the physiotherapy centre but nothing worked. I was going through a tough time in my relationship with my girlfriend and in retrospect, it shocks me that a small sprain didn't get cured for almost two years. Our feet, especially ankles, are very small parts of our body but support our entire weight. They are so crucial that our whole body can fall to the ground if they lose grip. Support is the key here as the ankles reflect the support we depend on, not just from others, but from our inner support system as well. This inner system consists of the psychological and emotional self-belief that gives our lives meaning and purpose.

I was continuously living in doubt, questioning myself and had almost nothing to hold on to. I realised that this happens when we go through some kind of tremor, extreme pain, and feeling of rejection or feel cheated and think that we cannot stand alone on our own. In my case, my own beliefs were being questioned. My own inner support system was letting me down. A broken ankle represents a very deep conflict with the ground, that is, the idea you are standing on and support for where you are going. I started questioning my own underlying belief regarding my relationship that was damaging my ability to stand up for myself. Our ankles allow us flexibility of movement. I found out through my research that sprained or twisted ankles indicate a lack of flexibility for the direction we're going in. I realised that I was being pulled in different directions and needed to change where I was headed. I accepted the relationship and did not disconnect or discard it. I instead became aware of my feelings and started seeing their source.

A few days later somebody told me to revisit the physiotherapist and with just seven days of exercising my ankle got completely cured. It seems when you are emotionally calm and centred and aligned with your purpose of life, god or as I say, nature, sends its messengers to guide you in the right direction. All such pains in my body soon became the best sources that caught me unaware and helped me see the emotions behind the pain. Ask yourself what needs your attention in your life to redirect to what you are avoiding or struggling to deal with. Notice your unconscious thought patterns and deal with the emotions produced powerfully. If you have wisdom to know and understand, you will be free from all pain. If you perceive a threat, the body's self-defence system will kick in and give rise to unexplained aches and pains.

Davis Suzuki wrote in *The Sacred Balance* that "condensed molecules from breath exhaled from verbal expressions of anger, hatred and jealousy contain toxins. Accumulated over one hour, these toxins are enough to kill 80 guinea pigs!" We get so trapped in our egoistic thinking that we don't even realise the harm we do to our bodies when we indulge our negative emotions and unprocessed experiences that then spread throughout the body.

Affected Adult Relationships

Believe it or not, our childhood affects our relationships and how we interact with others even later in life. If we were loved and cared appropriately when we were kids, we will most likely exhibit the same traits as adults. If we were abused and neglected, we will most likely develop characteristics to protect ourselves as adults such as being defensive or overly protective.

When I was a youngster, I stayed almost always angry and struggled with long-term relationships personally and professionally, which lead to a series of short-term and unstable relationships. It is important for me to mention that not every child with emotionally unavailable friends or parents will develop into an adult with problems. Some adults develop into better people than their peers could ever be. Every situation is different and the variables in the lives of children with emotionally lacking relationships are also different. However, for the most part, children with an emotional void often develop into teenagers and adults with problems that they themselves cause due to a lack of consciousness. Still, no child deserves to be rejected. We can and should encourage children to be kind and tolerant of others, and let them know that cruelty is never acceptable. Helping children with off-putting behaviours recognize and change these if possible will reduce their problems when they grow up.

Pattern of Feeling Rejected

When you feel rejected and it registers in the memory, it becomes a huge emotional block. The mind's purpose is to take information in and make decisions based on that information. The moment the ego interprets that the situation or what has been said has a link with it, emotions are produced. All links come from the past. If the link is not established, humans won't experience any emotions. If someone else loses his car keys, it does not impact us as much as when we lose ours. When someone rejects me, my block of being rejected surfaces.

I was possessed by my pattern of "feeling rejected". Many times I felt it was impossible to get out of my own defunct perception. I was living inside my own stories. I knew I was increasing the negativity myself and making it difficult to come out of it. Knowing that you are caged in your own heavy emotions when you try to escape is possibly the first step.

Recently I was staying in a hotel just after demonetization in India. I requested the hotel manager to give me Rs. 2,000 cash by swiping my card. I didn't find his response positive and I started feeling reactive. I could sense the volatile energy inside starting to wriggle out through my words and behaviour. My thoughts had begun to spiral out of control. How can I avoid the hotel manager's "no" plaguing me? The ego had already started triggering the emotional pattern within me, the old memories of feeling rejected were coming to the fore once again. However, at that moment I realised that it's not important who you are but it is what you do during such times that makes you *who you are*. We detect threats as per our conditioning. I did nothing in the situation; I acknowledged the workings of the ego and the feelings subsided. I realised that you can feel the ego spring and if you become aware, it dissipates and vanishes completely.

We need to change the villain (ego) in our stories and fortify the hero (consciousness).

Being Aware of the Emotional Blocks in Action

I was talking to a friend in a very pleasant environment. My friend mentioned something about his friend and how he had helped him. All of a sudden I started talking to him harshly, my voice became shrill and I started blaming him for something very minor. He asked me what the matter was, I said it's nothing but at the same time I was feeling the anger inside telling me that everything is wrong. I did not even maintain proper eye contact with my friend after my reaction as I knew that my hostility will be revealed to him. I was feeling a sense of tremendous hatred towards him. I forgot everything and spoke as if I was talking to an unknown person, absolutely cold.

For the first time I realised how these emotional blocks establish themselves and how they completely take over our personalities. Whatever I was feeling was from past hurts, which had become my reality. My reaction was based on a past incident where my friend didn't ask me if I wanted some help when I was in dire need of support. I had already spoken to him about this once but it wasn't enough I suppose, and I kept trying to forget the exact details of what I had felt bad about. Therefore, this incident kept raising its ugly head, spoiling my relationship with my friend till I came face to face with the emotional blocks from my own past.

When we develop a habit of not expressing feelings and burying them under the carpet, the pain remains and keeps coming to the fore when you least expect it. These emotional blocks coupled with the ego make us who we are NOT and we ACT on the basis of that! So we don't think right and the emotions produced are all false, thus making us act out in such a dramatic manner.

Emotional States Can't Be Hidden

Whenever I would get under the influence of the ego, many of my friends would look at me and ask, "Shashank, is everything alright, you look tensed?" I would be surprised at their questions because personally I didn't know that I had been taken over by the ego and was under the impression that I was being meditative rather than being reactive. I would then react as if they asked something very insulting. Howsoever hard we try, our emotional states can't be hidden. We exude energy that corresponds to our inner states. Many people sense it subconsciously, not knowing our inner state, but they definitely react to what they sense unknowingly. They won't respond to what we say but what they feel about us. The fact is that majority of us don't understand this and keep wondering why people react to us in a particular way, even when we are talking sense. I'm sure at one point or the other we have all met people who emanate strong negative emotional energy and whatever they say doesn't make any difference to what we feel about them.

So in my case, neither were my friends wrong, as they could see my emotions reflected on my face clearly and feel my strong negative energy, nor was I, as my consciousness was asleep, making my being (my true nature) dead. Many times I was absent-minded, which simply meant present somewhere else. I would not pay attention to the present situation and I would be present to what my ego was telling me, looking for evidence to prove that nobody loved me. I would feel lonely and unfulfilled. Wherever I went, would not be the right place, where I wanted to be. This made me angry and sad. I would react to my father, mother, sister, brothers, boss and friends even for the slightest of deviations from expectations. The ego is looking from the past, for the past and wanting the past in the present which does not exist. The ego itself is a non-existing entity so whatever it looks for, it cannot find, as the ego itself doesn't exist.

I'm an extrovert, but whenever my ego took over, I would run away from people. I would try to complete meetings in a hurry, avoid friends, put the phone down in a rush and experience immense impatience.

My only unconscious agenda was to impress people and look good.

I went to astrologers to find out what was happening to me. I started measuring my worth using the money I had. I started feeling that people didn't respect me because I had very little money, which is often true with similar egocentric personalities, but in my circle, people around me actually respected me. But I did not feel the respect as I was absent to them and present to what my ego saw and wanted. In such cases, I could hear the ego saying, "My way or the highway. You cannot screw me any longer." This was the voice of the ego, not mine. I was getting screwed without even a screwdriver.

The Ego Determines the Degree of Hurt

When you are in the clutches of the ego, you tend to get hurt very easily and as a result end up hurting others. Ego wants to get even and keeps you engaged in its automated thinking. That is its survival mechanism. It even works on imaginary thoughts. I would mentally keep replying to people almost all the time and feel drained. When you watch a film, you know that it's just a projection, but if you take a look at people in the theatre after watching a sad film, you will be surprised to see that everybody's handkerchiefs are wet. Emotions are the body's response to thoughts and it cannot distinguish between what's real and imaginary. On the other hand, this also opens up the possibility of managing emotions on your own volition, by managing thoughts consciously and not just leaving them unobserved to drive our life. If left unobserved, our whole life turns into a pursuit of seeking attention and love in the garb of earning money and respect. The funny part is, we are trying to earn money to buy love, which is available for free. The more you give, the more you get. The currency for buying love is not notes but simply giving back what you want to begin with, love and care. You can give only once you drop the ego because people who are egocentric will always give to get which is actually not giving at all.

Love, Nature's Language

When you keep operating from feelings, you use nature's language. Nature works with the language of love, that's why we all are born in a loving environment. Human beings are the weakest when they are born and cannot survive without love and care, unlike many animals. Remembering this, when you listen with feelings, you can easily see other people's feelings as well. Notice that more than you want money, you want appreciation and love. To get love you feel that you need money as you have experienced that people who have money are well respected. But love doesn't happen in the domain of receiving but in giving. Once experienced, love is forever, unlike money. Money once experienced creates the desire for more. Love, on the other hand, is complete in itself. There is no more to it because it is not quantifiable in terms of measurement. It is quantifiable when you start accepting, surrendering and giving. It has the power to transform you. The very presence of someone in love is transforming but if it's love for a particular thing then it's not love. It's your mind fulfilling what the heart lacks. When you don't have love on the inside, it becomes love for a particular thing. Money becomes important as that is the only currency to buy the external. Money is important, not as a centre but as an outcome of the presence of consciousness, your centre.

Consciousness Technique: For those who can't feel, slow down on your thoughts. Don't think incessantly. Stop and check the quality of your thoughts. You stop; don't try to stop the thought. Stopping will only move the thought from the conscious to the unconscious and it will start becoming stronger and keep repeating in your mind.

Egoistic Thinking is Repetitive, So Are Emotions

Since the ego runs on past memories stored in the unconscious, its chatter is repetitive. Majority of the thinking that we do is involuntary, automatic and without any purpose. Voluntary thinking is when you have the power to stop it when you want to and have a say in your thinking. So emotions too are mechanical, as are your thoughts. The problem with thinking too much is, it goes on till the time you intervene consciously, as does the production of uncontrolled emotions. So many people are unable to stop it and live almost their entire life in the clutches of the intense feeling of remorse, guilt, anger and hatred. It is as if they are possessed by some witch and keep doing what the witch tells them to do.

We come across many people who are victims of this witch; I personally have been one. People who are taken over by the ego, the witch, primarily look disconnected with themselves and with the people around them. It's not that they are disconnecting on purpose but it's because of their unconsciousness that they remain absent to themselves and their surroundings.

Negative Emotions and the Childhood Connection

Negative emotions primarily come from conditioned responses which may spring from an unhappy childhood and include persistent thoughts like:

- Nobody loves me.

- Nobody accepts me.

- Nobody respects and appreciates me.

- Nobody wants to play with me.

- Nobody wants to associate with me.

When someone perpetually remains glued to these thoughts, they suffer continuously. Their whole view towards life comes from these belittling thoughts looking for evidence of acceptance all the time. And as they say, you inadvertently find what you are looking for. Those who are always conscious of how people are treating them or what the situation of their life is remain defensive. They keep finding more and more incriminating evidence. They are self-conscious, not conscious. "Self" is the ego here. Instead of enjoying life, their whole focus is on surviving it. If they greet their boss and he does not return the greeting, the next thought that they will have is, "Even the boss doesn't love me." Now the boss might himself be preoccupied with the thought, "Nobody respects and appreciates me" and when someone is actually doing it, the boss too may not be present to the demonstration of respect and love. This is what is happening in the world. People are rarely aware of the reality. Almost everybody is stuck with the ego and not conscious to the present.

Past Upsets Affect the Present

One is often upset because of the past upsets and not because of his present circumstances. Present circumstances just act as a trigger. People become ticking bombs and the moment their ego perceives a threat, they explode. Our whole life is feeling-based, all our decisions stem from feelings and if we don't learn to have positive emotions, we will have a tough time even surviving, forget about enjoying.

I am reminded of an incident where I was having a fight with my sister. I was speaking to one of my clients over the phone and my sister came inside the room and started talking to me. I got so angry that I felt like hanging up and giving her a piece of my mind. But she understood that I was getting angry and left the room. After a while my mother came in and she too said something but this time I asked my client to hold on for a minute and replied to my mother. I didn't get irritated at all, in fact, I even shared what my mother was talking about with my client. I realised that we are never upset because of what is happening right now, we get upset because of the past upsets that we carry. I came to terms with the fact that I was somewhere not okay with my sister and it was that unresolved conflict that had triggered me and not her interruption. What are you doing is not important, where it is coming from is.

Are you someone who is almost always filled with envy, anger, jealousy, cruelty, brutality, sadness and pain? Does it take just one scratch for your real self to come out? One comment from someone and you blow things out of proportion? The moment someone says something that does not match your thinking, do you get defensive and angry? It is so because you remain childish till you don't stop living in an absolute lack of self-knowledge. Living a great life is an art and cannot be learnt by attending any number of "Art of Living" courses.

Any other understanding of you is just a fiction and not the truth. For example you may think about yourself as a calm and relaxed person but what you actually do when your expectations break, somebody insults you, when your wife talks to another man, or when your assumptions fail and your belief is shattered is who you actually are.

The thought that you are a calm and relaxed person is merely the voice in your mind, it's not you. To understand yourself, you have to have a two-sided view; one, your relationships outside and two, your inner dialogue that is always on. This understanding about yourself is not going to be an intellectual process or accumulation of knowledge, rather it is learning about yourself.

Notice that people who are sad and sorrowful are those who have accumulated knowledge about themselves and their mistakes instead of learning from their mistakes and those of others. Knowledge comes from the past but learning happens in the now and you are always fresh in the present. People keep gathering information about themselves and others and stay burdened beneath that whole frame of memories. Their mind keeps noting the mistakes they do, keeps noting the mistakes others do and keeps reacting to those.

The ego remains in a rut, repeating the same thing in view to have authority and therefore learns only that which empowers it further. Thus no new learning takes place as new learning can happen only from moment to moment, being present.

Memory keeps throwing at you the areas of potential threats, and the mind, with its thoughts, keeps replying. Once I asked for a glass of milk and the person concerned forgot. I scolded her very badly. The moment I did that, my attention went to myself. I observed myself. The very act of observing started transforming my anger and I started feeling calm because of the insights I gathered; the insight was eye-opening. It wasn't that person who made me angry, in fact, I was angry from before. She just became the medium. The trigger could have been anything or anyone else, even a fly or a cockroach.

I started drilling my memory for the trigger and it came to me like a flash of lightning. Five minutes prior, I was sitting peacefully in my drawing room looking at the flowers on the balcony. I was looking at the plants and started feeling a little uncomfortable. I felt anger welling up inside me and started feeling tense. I paid attention to what was going inside my mind and I noticed a thought that said, "I had given Rs. 500 to my neighbour and he has not returned it". Now after this thought, a chain of suggestions and comments began coming in one after the other.

"Now I will never give money to him"

"How can he do this?"

"I'll go and ask him for Rs. 500"

"This man is threatening, he can ask for more money in the future."

Meanwhile, the milk incident happened and the medium changed from my neighbour to the person who forgot to get me milk. I acted upon the feeling created by the thought. I was feeling uneasy and because of that I reacted and my tone, behaviour and words became aggressive. I started hurting her without knowing the truth, I was reduced to a puppet of the ego, totally unconscious and unaware of what I was doing.

The moment I became conscious and was able to observe my thoughts and feelings, the frequency of the thoughts reduced and finally they disappeared altogether and the feelings, too, vanished.

I realised that it's not what happens to us that gives us pain but what we do with it that leads to the pain. The mind, in order to get our attention to the areas it fears, keeps reminding us about the dangers it sees. Since we don't know the art of handling our mind and its thoughts, it keeps repeating and this repetition becomes stress. Let's take a "feed-forward" instead of *feedback* from the mind to build a new future which is not coloured by the past. When you will be able to observe the movement of your inner energy, they will start transforming by your intentions.

The moment the master of the mind is there in control – that is you – you can tell your mind to think what you want and the mind will acquiesce and you will be out of the trap. This reclamation of your mastery over your mind is the whole idea behind getting to the source of creation and getting out of reacting.

If you see yourself through your achievements or possessions, you will miss the reality. Many times possessions and achievements can be a mere result of your inheritance, intellectual capacity, knowledge about the work you do or a right move made at the right time.

Words cannot describe the kind of mind we have, but our attention to and awareness about how we speak, feel, communicate, carry ourselves, walk and think do. The easiest way to see your mind is to see what you do in your relationships, what kind of intentions you have for the people around you. You might be having good relations with your friend but if you feel from inside that he is an idiot or that she is not a good person then you know that you are a hypocrite.

To know all this, you have to see yourself, observe yourself very keenly. We cannot know ourselves completely from the way we think about ourselves but seeing how creative we are in action, how we handle difficult situations, what we do when someone asks for help, are we caring enough, how others feel around us, whether we are fulfilling our responsibilities or simply blaming situations, people and trying to get away certainly helps in getting the big picture. Have I found something original inside me or am I just trying to impress others by acting the way they want me to be?

At times you have relations with people you don't approve of. This tells you a lot about your commercial mind. When you accept your parents with their weaknesses, it tells you that you are becoming mature. When your boss makes a mistake and you have the courage to not say anything and very politely try to help him, then know that you are growing in life. If you criticise your boss or friends, blame your parents, complain about the company, it shows that you are avoiding being responsible. To see yourself is to see who you are in your relationships. There is no other way to get to know yourself.

Once I experimented with an executive from a multinational company who had this massive problem with his job, the people and systems around him and the way his life was. He kept on complaining about the environment and the people around him being responsible for his sorrowful state of affairs. I told him to make a mood journal for seven days, every hour for eight hours. He did it very earnestly and came to me explaining the various causes of his sorrow and how people were not letting him live properly. I told him to go to a hill station and spend time there in isolation and continue writing the mood journal. He was surprised when I showed him that he felt sad and bad at almost same time when he was surrounded by people. Our minds become programmed to produce certain emotions on the basis of certain triggers that the mind associates itself with. Even when the trigger is not there, the thoughts that are repeating constantly in the mind produce the same response at the same time.

You should observe yourself without any external factors, even when you are alone, see whether or not you are the same person who is with people and situations. There should be no difference. This is how you get to know yourself. This is actually learning through observing. We keep gathering information and knowledge as to what happened with us, who did it, who was responsible, why they did it rather than seeing that it's our own mind which is making us feel the way we feel. It's your ongoing thinking that is the problem. This constant nonsensical thinking can stop only when we are awake, that is, conscious by taking charge of the mind.

Also observe how many of you make your bodies insensitive by drinking, smoking and overeating, consuming these toxic substances, deteriorating the quality of your attention, making it dull. So if your bodies are dull, you cannot have an alert mind, or an alert consciousness. It will keep forcing you to do things which, it feels, will give you pleasure and help you avoid pain. The best thing about consciousness is, when you are present you just can't do something which is not good for you and even others for that matter. The very presence of consciousness is the absence of the mind, that is the past and the future, so all the actions come from the present moment's needs.

Observe what makes you feel bad after taking action – it may be your behaviour, attitude, action or intention. Whatever is disturbing you requires attention. Any disturbance shows you that you are operating from the mind. For example, you get angry with your son or maid, and after a while you feel, "I should not have used such harsh words". Being present will help you avoid, by default, harsh words, enable you to speak in a nice tone and give you the confidence to express what you don't like in an amicable manner rather than by demeaning and cutting people.

Unless you can see yourself for who you are inside, you are asleep. Your eyes may be open but your soul is asleep and till the time you open your inner eyes, you will continue to be controlled by the mind. Keep observing your mind and how it keeps you in a dreamlike state. It keeps telling you that one day your boss will change, your company will change, your spouse will change, you will have more money and then everything will be alright. Your mind simply does not want to see the reality which is as it is right now. You can wake up only if you see the present moment and its impact on you.

To observe is to wake up for action.

Discover Your Triggers to Get Emotionally Smart

Unwanted feelings like anger, fear, hurt, sadness, etc., get triggered from past experiences that have been repressed. It happens so unconsciously that even a person, a particular situation, a strong smell, song or colour may trigger you. The ego is so clever that when it gets activated it may deflect your feelings and blame another person or the situation. All trigger-based reactions are fear-based, having low vibrational frequencies. A majority of our reactions are masked as anger but they come from fear, we do this to protect ourselves from feeling hurt. For many of us anger becomes the main defence mechanism. It is necessary to remove anger and all other negative emotions having a high energy density out of our bodies in order to attract positive experiences.

Personally, my threat was not the fear of death but the fear of being unloved, unwanted, rejected and left out. The brain, which was programmed for survival from physical threats of animals in the past, has shifted to threats about people and respectability. My experience has taught me that you are good only when people accept you and people accept you only when you are intelligent. Now not only do I try to get accepted by people but also do all kinds of things that show how intelligent I am. Now the interesting part is, normally people feel accepted when they think they have enough money but this does not make a difference to me as my mind is trained to stay happy irrespective of the money I have. Now even seeing someone buying a Mercedes or building a mansion in my circle does not provoke me to buy one for myself. But if these people didn't invite me or if I felt neglected by even their gestures, I used to get triggered. As we get attached to our requirements, our brain constantly looks to ensure that we have them, despite various circumstances and gets threatened the moment it feels we might not get them. This way our needs become emotional triggers.

While going for a training program in a college, my colleague got late because of a task that I myself had assigned her. She was to get a few notes photocopied and I knew it would take time. She was five minutes late. I left her and went for my training program. I reached 30 minutes before the scheduled time but since I got annoyed just by her coming late, my emotional block got triggered and I reacted. Now, in hindsight, I can locate the source. Once our whole family was going for a movie and I was very young, maybe ten years old. Just before going, I felt like I had to go to the washroom. I went and when I came back my father had already left with the whole family leaving me behind. From that day, I not only made it a point to be on time or communicate when I am going to be late but also began expecting others to be on time. Punctuality became a major reason for my dormant emotional blocks to get active.

Another trigger that was instilled in me is quite common with many people.

I had developed claustrophobia as my elder brother had locked me in the toilet when I was small and did not switch on the lights. It was very dark; I was in the toilet crying like crazy for almost half an hour. Since then till the time I worked on myself, I felt very uncomfortable in lifts, flight toilets and at concerts as I also felt claustrophobic in huge crowds. As I continued my quest into human behaviour, I realised that the present moment may be difficult to handle but the past moments stored in the mind make the present impossible to handle.

Difficult and Triggering People Can Actually Help Awaken Us

Like us, other people too have their emotionally blocked energy and when they react, our blocks get reactivated very easily. There are many people who regularly go through violent and emotionally charged situations almost on a daily basis. Recently I had applied for a loan in one of the leading banks of India. The executive who had come to explain the details had a very strong negative energy emanating from him and made me feel very uncomfortable. I immediately felt the need to remove myself from the room and reduce my interaction with him. I was actually feeling disgusted by his energy field and felt aggressive. His negativity was somewhere triggering my hidden negativity.

> When a person high on ego is encountered, he should be respected. These people are actually our teachers who pose as testing grounds for our awareness level and inner muscles. For us, these people are important to check whether we get impacted by them or not. If we get impacted or find their presence disturbing then there is more for us to learn and further awareness needs to be developed.

I was practicing 'being present' now for quite some time and had been waiting for such opportunities to keep practicing. I told this gentleman that one of the other banks was giving me better rates than his bank. This triggered him and he started speaking at a higher pitch as if threatening me. It could have very easily created a conflict but I remained in my consciousness and just started observing my energy. The moment I did that, the energy that was just about to get activated stopped immediately and I started looking at him with a very polite smile, not being taunting or hostile. This conscious change in my state somewhere broke his flow of negative energy. I was feeling very calm and powerful and he too may have sensed that unconsciously and all of a sudden his whole voice and body language changed. He became calm and gentle. Instead of forcing me, he started working with me towards negotiating the best deal. I felt, stepping out of the voice in my head, the ego and its reflection on my body was not at all felt by me. I experienced an inner ease that normally the thinking mind cannot understand and keeps misinterpreting by reading to other people. The ego believes in blaming others always by saying, "You don't care that's why you talk like this; you don't help me when I need it; you hate me." When you are present you relate at a much deeper level than the ego's voices in your head.

People who carry heavy emotionally blocked energy can be triggered by anything, right from not getting their slippers in the morning to not getting a promotion in the office. Many people's ego doesn't even allow them a holiday from their self-created sufferings because of these blocks. They even work on Sundays to suffer.

The Camouflaged Emotional Block

I remember a friend's father; he always had a smile and spoke very politely, almost as if the man was enlightened. But his emotional block and massive ego were so evident that you could clearly see the violence in his eyes. It seemed he was fooling only himself by pretending that everything was smooth in his life but everybody else could clearly see that nothing, absolutely nothing was working out in his life. He was so aggressive; I could clearly see that he was just waiting for the next person to shout at. He would take pride in shouting and then would all of a sudden become quiet and smiling. The ego in him was always trying to show how much he had the situation under control. People who show that they are in control and relaxed are often the ones who can murder someone on the slightest of triggers as they shove everything inside while trying to prove that they are the best. Because of their emotional blocks they blow up trivial issues out of proportion. The worst part is that these people are not aware of the pain inside and project their suffering on the situation and other people. These people cannot differentiate between the event and their reaction to the event. Their reaction makes the event big or small. These people are so highly egoistic and unconscious that they don't even know that they spend their entire life justifying themselves.

Many times such people are right but because of the blocked and negative emotional energy in them, they keep giving rise to enemies who are triggered by their unconsciousness. The egos of such people not only fight with outsiders but also keep creating enemies at home.

Staying Emotionally Complete

Anything left incomplete will keep lingering in you and your mind will keep ticking like a time bomb. When I hang up the phone abruptly, I feel incomplete. If I don't bid farewell properly before leaving a party, something inside me keeps telling that I have missed something. If I hurt somebody knowingly there is unease and something inside urges me to apologize.

People who hurt you may realise their folly on their own and come back to you one day or the other. If they don't come back and you keep waiting, you will suffer from emotional blocks. Be careful because the mind always tries to hurt those who hurt you, so if you reply to them with hurt and anger, they don't see what they did in the first place but are ready to hurt you again in response to what you do. If you are aware to begin with, you won't get hurt, as it is the ego that gets hurt. Getting stuck will keep you incomplete. Forgive people by seeing their side of the story. Getting stuck means continuing to operate from the past hurt. Your past hurts are nothing but an inner perception coming from lack of wisdom and knowledge. Once you are hurt and a block is formed, even a thought about that triggers things. When I was hurt by my friends, of course because of my own misinterpretations, their invitation for a party too used to provoke me. I had to put in a lot of efforts to go there and stay calm. Attending parties became a struggle till the time I dealt with my issues with them and became aware of my unconsciousness and habitual pattern of complaining. Whatever grudges I had, I told them and took responsibility for what I was feeling.

I still don't meet them frequently but this time it's not because I want to avoid them but because I want to spend more time with myself.

I realised that life cannot possibly be altered by fixing and changing other people and even if you are a master fixer and succeed in fixing this one person or situation, the very next moment you will encounter the same resistance from a different person and in a different situation. What we experience is not their resistance but our own resistance reflecting in them.

So as my inner journey to growth and development began, I imbibed this in me and started communicating openly with people. I would not keep anything in my heart but started expressing it then and there before an image gets formed. I started completing my interactions and the inner dialogues that used to stress me vanished completely. Wherever I found my energy leaking due to the inner chattering of thoughts, I started plugging it. Initially, I avoided everybody to see what the matter was. I used to feel very uncomfortable with my own family and friends. I started avoiding them till the time I realised that avoidance itself is a part of the ego. With my inner development, acceptance of others also started happening. I noticed my spiritual development as my reactions started becoming calm and composed. No one can hurt you if the "want" is not there. Say, for example, you are going to a party and you don't set any expectations in your mind from people and just go with the flow. You will be yourself and living in the moment will make you creative. When you are yourself, people connect with you as deep down we are all one. When we try to impress others or base our actions on a past hurt, it's not us who is operating but the ego. That's why people cannot relate to us when there is a wall of inhibitions in the form of the ego.

I spoke to my friends and told them that I had been indulging in various idiotic acts and atrocities that my ego had made me do, which of course helped me in becoming self-aware and writing this book. But I realised that others don't know this and see us the way we behave with them. So there needs to be a completion exercise where we express what we are feeling. It is not like asking for forgiveness but involves expressing everything that you feel inside. Initially, my friends didn't take it nicely as I had blamed them earlier and I too did not feel comfortable somewhere inside. Though it felt light initially, after some time I started having those thoughts of criticising and condemning people again. I finally told them that this was a pattern, my insecurities that shoot from feeling rejected right from my childhood which surfaced over and over again. The moment I explained it to them in this manner and took responsibility rather than blaming others, I became free.

So it's not really a problem of people or situations, it's a problem of our outlook, the way we see people, situations and the world. There is nothing new that you can interpret, as all interpretations are from the past. So what you really get is a bit of yourself when you interpret them. It's about us being complete. To be complete and powerful, we can simply alter the person's perception by altering our interpretation of them. Altering the way the other person is perceived by you is the best way to alter your behaviour towards them, because your behaviour is directly correlated with the way the other is perceived by you. Good behaviour saves time and reduces conflicts.

People think that if they have money, other people will respect them. It is not money that gets us respect or makes us feel confident but the confidence that creates the money and the respect. Cheerful surroundings do not make one happy. It is being happy that leads to cheerful surroundings. Unfortunate circumstances only show up to bring to the fore your pre-existing state of unhappiness and under confidence. The moment you are complete from within, you experience happiness as an outcome of getting rid of your incompletion and people love to connect with you.

Whatever you are hiding is driving your life. Just go and express what you feel to your boss, friends, wife, parents and even people as seemingly unimportant as your servant. Anything you will hide will take the driving seat of your perceiving mechanism and start seeing things from there. Just become whole. Talk to people, express, share what you feel and get it over with. Detached from the negative energy is the presence of positive energy. Getting your inner feelings out by releasing them through the walls of conditioning and programming is called freedom. Just keep in mind the way you express yourself should not be offensive or hurtful. The problem lies in hiding your feelings.

The Way of the Wizard

People start transforming in your eyes the moment you find out what was causing them to act in a particular way. You interpreted them a certain way before and when you change that, they appear transformed to you. They don't do anything hostile or negative but rather reflect what you have done or tend to do.

Taking genuine care of people is as good as healing them. So it is better that you start working on the ego, which stands as a barrier between genuine connections and makes your life hell. The misery you are living in is the hell that tells you about your ego, about your expectations and what needs to be corrected. So there is no such thing as tough times, only doors towards the purpose of your life which are tough to open. Clues required for improvement are always available from your interactions with people and from the situations that come in your life and the way you react to them.

How to Dissolve Emotional Blocks

No event or other person can affect you emotionally without your consent. It is impossible.

The first step hence is to become aware of heavy emotions, the moment they become active. Reasons start surfacing as a result of your consciousness:

- There is always a judgment about some situation. For example, when someone betrays you.

- The moment you evaluate the situation as "this is bad for me", negative emotions arise. If you evaluate it consciously, focusing on *what is* rather than on *why me*, no negative emotions are produced. Of course, you will feel bad if someone breaks your trust or God forbid someone dies but it won't turn into an emotional block that makes you suffer your entire life.

- There are certain bodily manifestations of these emotions: you experience various sensations such as a burning sensation in your chest, stomach or a feeling of tightness in your back or throat. These can be different for different people. If you do physical exercises regularly, these bodily symptoms too subside over a period of time.

When you avoid reacting to the initial symptoms, the blocks don't get any energy from your attention, slowly loosen their grip on you, eventually fading away.

A written log is always helpful in spotting the right emotion:

The Troublesome emotion	What judgment on your part caused the emotion	How you evaluated it	How did you feel	What are your thoughts/ what are you saying about it.

A majority of our triggered responses arise from evaluating unknown future consequences. Consciousness breaks the identification and the emotional blocks cannot control your thinking any longer. They start losing their energy, though it takes a little time. You feel free from the past, as it no longer distorts your present perceptions. The energy that was consumed by the emotional blocks becomes available for use in the present. People who are chronically depressed and anxious sometimes doubt if they can change their outlook and become habituated to thinking negative thoughts. The trick lies in your willingness to change your thought pattern and the more you do it, the better you become. You can control all the voices in your head, that is, how you think and interpret situations.

Once you realise that you have emotional blocks and become present the moment they get triggered, you will start becoming even more aware. Emotional blocks then will become a guiding post to consciousness as the moment they will arise, you would know what to do. Do nothing, but just be a witness of them without identifying which is like giving food to them. Over a period of time, you will be completely free of them, as you keep getting free from the ego which keeps them alive.

When we are angry, upset or anxious, we are likely to make errors in judgment and the way we think. We may see all the angles but everything looks unclear as the lens of perception gets foggy. Because of this we are unable to know the truth and jump to conclusions about people, events, situations and even ourselves. Once we learn that we have a distorted perception, we can change the lens and see things as they are in reality.

I had a fight with my father once. Even though we resolved it, whenever I would go to meet him, at a sub-conscious level, something would get triggered. I realised that working at the thought level is not sufficient and you have to remove the emotional charge of the past memories by transforming who you are as a person. You can be yourself by expressing what you feel, needless to say, in a non-reactive manner. I shared this with my father who suggested me to just eat something tangy or spicy the moment I start feeling this way. It works to alter the thought and be rational and from there you can take it up by being present. Another thing I did was, I also started ignoring those thoughts and remained in the present while making affirmations; that is, reducing the ego's negativity with positive self-talk and altering non-optimal and dysfunctional thought patterns. These positive messages tend to work as emotional currency because they give you new energy along with mental peace and facilitate better coping skills to deal with your situations. They change your outlook and perception.

For example, whenever negative thoughts clouded my mind

regarding the clash with my father, I started saying to myself the following statements:

"I love my self."

"I love my father."

"I am the best."

I also did one simple thing, I started estimating the truth of the situation whenever I got triggered by emotions. This made me aware, and I asked myself, "Am I losing anything right now or not? Is my father actively denying me something that I need or am I taking the situation personally?"

The answer that I got was, first, "If it's true that my father is ignoring any of my needs or stopping me from achieving it, I will ask for what I need. Second, if it doesn't really matter, then I should drop the painful idea that he is making me suffer and move on." Without consciously acknowledging what is triggering the emotional reaction, we become enslaved to our needs and react badly to the person we think is standing in between.

If we authentically tell people what we feel, about our needs and how we had expected them to treat us in a particular way then we can see life more objectively. With people who you are close to, you can tell them that some particular words/statements trigger you and you can both take care so that it doesn't ruin the relationship. Being frank about your triggers not only makes you authentic but also develops trust in people. From this perspective, we are always free to choose our reactions, as they won't be one-sided. This will develop self-knowledge, enable you to see your blocks clearly and help you understand that it is never the current situation that makes you react but the emotional block. This consciousness will make you present of the egoistic energy that starts building up. Being present will not let you identify with this energy and will not also let the witch of negativity possess you.

Ignore and Refuse to Answer the Egoistic Mind

As soon as you realize that the ego is talking to you, refuse to engage in a conversation as you know that it will mislead you and affect your mood. Whenever you take decisions from a divided mind, you will notice that the moment you take a decision, the opposite always confuses you. If you decide to tell someone to stop doing something, the ego will catch hold of you and say, "You should not have done this." So it is better to ignore it completely when the ego tries to hook you. It's important to recognise that whenever you take a decision from the egoistic mind, you will always feel uneasy as it comes from the unconsciousness.

Check the Ego's Misinterpreted Calling

When you answer challenges unconsciously, your ego takes control over you. If you get present to any of the following, know for sure that your ego has misinterpreted something or is reacting on some already misinterpreted past:

Overgeneralizing, trying to be perfect, all or nothing mentality, filtering based on past or future insecurities, exaggerating rejection, having a negative outlook, magnifying/minimizing, trivializing events, stretching or shrinking your thinking, 'should' and 'ought' statements, mistaken identity, guilt and self-blame, forecasting yours and others' future, trying to read minds and jumping to conclusions.

Making Good Memories Creates Insights

All thoughts come from memories and memories are made from karmas. Karmas are actions that come from attachments. So when you keep shedding attachments, there is no memory as the action is pure, not contaminated and creates a factual memory. There is a difference between factual and psychological, emotional memory. For example, you missed your flight means you missed your flight and now have to figure out what has to be done next. This is factual, whereas psychological and emotional memories get created when you get into the "what if" mode – "What if I don't get the next flight, what if I don't reach on time, what if I lose my job?"

When there is no psychological memory, you don't have judgmental thoughts and you are able to see the facts as they are. When you can see facts, you get insights; insights come when there is no interfering thought. Working on these insights is what creates bliss. Insight comes from total perception and not only from your thoughts. Instead of getting rid of thoughts, be aware. Expecting that there will be no thieves is too idealistic. But policing yourself is realistic.

If someone has abused you 10 years ago, the incident goes into your memory and whenever you meet that person, thoughts of rejection rear up in your mind. This is psychological memory. Now factual memory is when you have the memory that he abused you but you don't have the emotional charge of that so you meet him normally. It's a fact that he abused you but if you let that fact form an image about that person then it becomes a psychological memory.

Allowing the Emotions to Be

Be sad when you feel sad. When the mind tries to be something other than what it is, there is struggle. Don't try getting out of mood swings, be with them, don't run away from them, face them and they will dissolve on their own. Feeling something is not the problem, trying to change how you feel is. Observing this movement of the mind is observation and leads to consciousness.

Sometimes accepting what is can be liberating!

Catharsis of Negative Emotions

Catharsis is a process of expressing pent up emotion to get out of the vicious cycle of egoistic thinking. If you express your anger to others, they will retaliate and another pattern of emotion will be added to your personality. Instead, learn to laugh at yourself, go to your room and beat a pillow. Go for a nice run being fully aware of your moments and take a hot or cold shower. If gripping negative emotional energy takes place easily then trust me, releasing it is even easier. It's just a matter of taking the first step towards freeing yourself from such self-punishing thoughts. Once the negative emotion is fully expressed, when you stop running from it and embrace it fully, go through it completely, it vanishes. Emotions are "energy in motion" and will freeze only if you make them freeze.

Right from childhood we are taught not to express strong emotions, cry or express ourselves in public, and instead to hide our emotions. We can see so many children being very aggressive as they don't know how to label their emotions, source the cause and channel them. This is existential suffering. Howsoever great your upbringing may be, you will still have to go through pain and suffering as the formation of the mind is the very root cause of broken expectations. And none of us have enlightened parents. The problem arises when people are not educated about the ego and feel this is what life is. As a matter of fact, suffering is the gateway to consciousness and the easiest way to get there.

Dropping the Past

A teacher did a beautiful exercise with her students once. She asked each child to get a few tomatoes in a plastic bag. She asked the children to write the name of a student they hated from their class on each tomato and put it back in the plastic bag. So when the day came, every child brought some tomatoes with the name of the student they hated. Some had five tomatoes, some had eight while some had up to twelve tomatoes. The teacher then told the children to carry the tomatoes in the bag with them wherever they go for 10 days. Time passed by and after a few days the children started complaining due to the horrible smell coming from the rotten tomatoes. Besides, some students also had to carry heavier bags because they had more tomatoes. After 10 days the children were relieved because the exercise had finally come to an end. The teacher asked, "How did you feel while carrying the tomatoes with you for 10 days?" The frustrated children complained of the trouble they had to go through carrying the heavy and smelly tomatoes wherever they went.

The hidden message told by the teacher was, "This is what happens when you carry negativity and hatred for others in your hearts. The stink of hatred and negativity will pollute your heart and you will carry it with you wherever you go. If you cannot tolerate the stench of spoilt tomatoes for just ten days, can you imagine what it is like to have the stench of hatred and negativity in your heart for an entire lifetime? We become so habituated to living in hatred that we are not able to, and sometimes are not willing to, let go even in painful situations, accumulating pain and suffering inside."

Over a period of time this pain becomes your personality. This persona comprises of negatively charged thoughts from emotions like anger, guilt, regret and resentment. A very strong ego gets developed as it identifies itself from what went wrong and results in an almost palpable energy demonstrated in our behaviour.

One can break this pattern of collecting hatred and get rid of it by simply not revisiting those thoughts. The problem comes when we become dead to alive people and alive to the dead past. When one, with little effort, starts staying in the present by being conscious, he is able to create a new personality from the present rather than sticking to the old rotten one, feeding like a scavenger on negative thoughts. The past has no power if you are conscious in the present moment. It impacts us only till the time we are present to it and absent to the present.

To change fate, look within; mend the bond broken by pride.

Signs of Freedom from Emotional Blocks

Freedom simply means the ability to pause between a thought and its response and seeing, before acting, whether that thought is coming from past experiences, hurts and future insecurities or is an insight from the present moment's awareness. It is very simple once you start practicing.

The moment I get free of some blocks, I lose weight, get rid of my toxins, have regular motions in the morning and become more creative and better at self-expression. And then my tolerance for everything increases multi-fold. Be it a messy table, your intrusive neighbour, the chilling winter... Nothing, absolutely nothing bothers you when you get rid of the emotional blocks. This is the state of consciousness. There comes a state of bliss in being in the midst of all this. Once you are free of ego, you will start enjoying your life and the human experience. It is not the body that is enjoying the soul's experience but the soul that is enjoying the bodily experience.

Ego-Generated v/s Natural Emotions from Being Conscious

Positive emotions that come from being conscious and natural have a very healing effect on the body, they even strengthen the immune system. However, ego-based positive emotions come with their opposites: love / hate, like / dislike, so on and so forth. If you love your sibling when they buy you gifts and hate them the very next moment when they wear some of your clothes, then this is ego-generated love. This kind of love comes from possessiveness and converts into hate the very next moment when the expectations break. Notice how people feel happy with praise and unhappy the next moment when someone condemns them. Emotions produced by ego come with its opposite, that's why with every good there comes a bad and every moment of happiness brings some unhappiness as well. Emotions generated by the ego are derived from the ego's identification with outside factors which are unstable and liable to change at any moment.

On the other hand, truly positive emotions result from a state of consciousness and are not transient emotions at all. They come from your state of being like love, joy and peace and are a part of your true nature. These emotions, rather states of being, don't have opposites and are not dependent on external factors. If you are happy because you have a Mercedes then that's an ego-generated emotion. If you feel joy with whatever you have or even do not have, then that's your state of being and nobody can take that away from you. As a matter of fact, true positive emotions can be experienced only when external factors are absent. Only in very rare cases do people experience inner bliss in the presence of physical comforts. That's why many rich people spend their entire lives wanting more and because of that suffer endlessly without any cure.

Creating an Empowering Context

The mind simply captures what it feels is threatening for you or what is good for you. It captures images for future reference and when any situation matching that image comes about, it provides what it had recorded earlier. It works in associations; this is why it is of paramount importance to create an empowering context to all challenges and unpleasant incidents. That is to say, avoid putting labels by condemning and criticising things and rather change the inner experience by changing the interpretation of the event itself. This way you have good memories and thoughts coming out of it.

A young, successful executive in his early-forties once came to one of my training programs. He looked strained and stressed despite all his success. On being grilled a little, he shared that as a baby he was found outside a temple wrapped in an orange bag. He said he has been frustrated throughout his life as he does not know who his parents are, who his mother is. He had been searching for his identity and his parents like a madman. I told him to create an empowering context for the same. I took his attention to what his mother did for him rather than seeing what she didn't. I told him "Imagine what condition your mother would have been in for her to leave you like this. But she still made sure to leave you at a public place where you were bound to be discovered and taken in."

The executive got it, and found his mother's love and care in that orange bag and in the act of leaving him outside the temple and developed respect for his mother instantaneously. This is called creating an empowering context. Now, earlier, the executive's life was filled with hatred and he operated from there. I just created a new story of love and care and brought it into his consciousness so that he could operate from there. It's just a matter of how you look at anything. If you develop the attitude of creating empowering contexts for any situation, you will always be powerful. Power is hidden in the way you look at things, situations, people and yourself. Notice that's why many negative people come across as powerful because they keep creating the right empowering contexts for their actions.

A Wrong Context Can Be Fatal

There was a boy who was in love with a young girl but the problem was his parents didn't approve of the girl and told him to never see that girl again. They said this very forcefully. The very next day the boy became blind. His mind couldn't make an empowering context and took the situation as it was, without seeing what else could be possible, and this made him go blind as he lost confidence from inside. The surprising part was, his eyes were absolutely alright as per the doctors but because of the psychological shock he became blind.

If one does not learn to be present then the ego interprets situations as per its own contexts which, a majority of the times, are counterproductive.

Once we were at our friend's place having dinner. I was on a weight-loss diet so I was eating salads and in my salad I got a piece of bitter cucumber. I ran to the washroom to spit it out and when I came back, one of my friends asked what happened. I said, "Nothing, just a bitter cucumber," to which he said, "Anything bitter is good for losing weight." I suddenly got a new empowering context and finished the entire plate including all the bitter cucumber.

Consciousness Technique

Keep ignoring old memories by creating new empowering contexts by not giving heed to that which is disturbing. Keep seeing the good in what happened or in the person whose thoughts disturb you.

The Context is Decisive and Not the Content

Cultivate an attitude of talking about positive things with those you complain about. Try to see positivity everywhere. Wherever there is hatred which you try to avoid, is also the area where you want to be free. It's important to get that the content of your mind is not you. It's the context that is decisive, that makes you who you are and not the content. Context is how we understand anything. If your father scolds you, instead of feeling insulted, create a new context by focusing on your inner energy field than on his scolding. The new context can be, "Maybe, he is in a bad mood or he is not in a position to understand right now, I will talk to him later." Keep it simple and don't create an emotional drain. Just a set of new eyes can change the whole view. Observe, whenever you encounter something you don't like, just change the context to a positive one. For example, you go through a divorce. Instead of feeling lonely, imagine all the time and energy you will have for peace and meditation. What has happened has happened but cribbing will only worsen what is left and you will be unable to recreate what is lost.

When Mahatma Gandhi was thrown off from that infamous train in South Africa because of the colour of his skin, he didn't react but rather created an empowering context around the incident thinking, "Now I will throw the British from my country and make sure that something like this never happens again." That is what great people do in the face of any eventuality. They take impetus and energy from it and channelize it in areas where they want to work and create results.

To alter the behaviour and actions, you need to alter your perception of the world because behaviour and action are perfectly correlated with the way the world occurs to you.

Transcending of Reaction

Ram, a participant at one of my training sessions, approached me one day and said, "I was travelling via Delhi Metro one day. When I got down it was almost 11pm and being a weekday, the train was almost empty. A rugged looking guy outside the station took out a gun and kept it on my forehead. He ordered me to take out all the money I had. I very obediently took out all the money and handed it over to him. When he started to leave, I told him,

'Hey listen, it is cold, why don't you take my jacket as well.' He was stunned but took my jacket. When he started going again, I called and said, 'Hey, you look hungry and I am hungry too. Do you want to eat something?' He had a grin this time and agreed to go with me. We had dinner together and started developing a sort of friendship. When the bill came, I told him that all my money was with him, so he should pay and he paid it. While departing I told him, 'According to the law of karma, when you take something from someone, you have to return it. So you have taken my money and jacket and eaten with my money so what do you wish to give me in return?' He said, 'What can I give?' I told him, 'See all these restaurants throw out surplus food in the evening, how about you help me collect it all as I run an NGO that collects the leftover food and distributes it to the poor.' He agreed and today we are not only good friends but also business partners." This is CONSCIOUS choice making, transcending YOUR OWN EGO, and the situation by just being calm and non-reactive, not just at the behaviour level but at the level of the consciousness.

Now let's look at what would have happened had he lost his cool. Ram gets into the metro train. This rugged-looking man takes out his gun and asks for money. Ram resists and tries to overpower the goon. The goon in this struggle fires the gun; Ram gets hit in the forehead and dies on the spot. Ram's family is left without a roof over their heads and the goon gets arrested by the police and finally is sent to the gallows. Both die and their families perish too. We lose a great NGO, which was helping so many people and providing food to so many poor people. People who got the food were able to live a life of dignity and maybe even started working and contributed to the GDP of the country.

So choose which option sounds more appealing and practical. The very choice leads to the awakening of the consciousness. Lowering your ego, getting out of the box, which is filled with resignation and cynicism or; being creative and expressing yourself with what you intuitively know. If you accept the challenge angrily then it's a reaction. If you accept the challenge gracefully, joyfully, willingly, it's a response.

When you are responsive to the ego of others, you not only dissolve your own ego but also help the other dissolve his. When you are aware, you can see that the reaction of the other person is stemming from the ego and you won't react as you know he is possessed and not present. This very response is enough to make the other person realise his reaction and make you independent from reacting.

A person who is free from dependence on others is also free from the fear of mistakes, rights and wrongs and has a very different quality of being. Then whatever he does is rhythmic and produces an optimum, holistic result which bestows peace and material success as well.

To do anything one requires a stable mind that comes from the right understanding.

I personally, when not present enough, avoid meeting people who operate from their egoistic minds. When I am taken over by my ego, which I can easily spot now, I am able to control many quarrels and fights, keeping friendship intact by staying away. When I am not present or rather when I am not conscious of my unconsciousness, my ego tries to find situations to react to. You can only see the situation calmly when you are present. When the ego is driving you, you can pretend to be calm by changing the attitude but it doesn't last long as the next situation is just around the corner.

"Everything that you are against weakens you. Everything you are for empowers you."

Recently I was returning from Delhi and the person just behind me in the plane was singing very loudly. I was listening to one of my tapes and got disturbed by his singing. There was an initial hitch and I wanted to tell him to stop. But I channelled my inner energy, so I focused on the tape and after sometime realised that I was not disturbed by his singing anymore. I looked at him and told him that he sings very well. Eventually, we became very good friends.

Earlier I used to react to such incidents and would be in conflict with people all the time. Almost daily one such incident used to happen and I would be stressed and annoyed all the time. I introspected to find that I look at the present through the lens of the disturbing past that hides within me. We are experiencing ourselves all the time. Sometimes the situations and people around us are definitely wrong but if we are responsive and aware, we don't increase the negative energy but rather try to calm it down.

I learnt that it is not possible to remove darkness by fighting with it. It is only light that can emerge victorious over darkness.

Consciousness Technique

See how you respond. If your way of looking at things is right then whatever life does to you will be right. You will enjoy everything, even your sadness. So be restless to get out of this permanent restlessness by finding your own truth, create your life and learn from mistakes. You don't have to go into guilt mode but see mistakes as opportunities. We all react as we are conditioned and it is okay. The moment you get conscious of this, the reactions stop on their own.

Clean up now, see things and situations as they are in reality and try to work with them and not against them. Use the force of the situation. Don't spend time proving each other wrong but work together to make things right. I learnt not to tell people that "you are like this – you are like that". Feedback is important at times but even more important is feeding them with positivity. Being critical creates negativity amongst others and in you. I also learnt not to cut people or interrupt them in their flow of work, thought or speech. Just accept others the way they are. Good communication and quality of relationships determine our lives to a great extent.

Distances shorten if reactions are absent.
If they are present, life shortens.

Inner growth happens only when you are absolutely unsatisfied with the way you are internally; your thoughts, feelings and intentions. Only then do you start rising higher, only then do you make efforts to pull yourself out of the dirt. This pulling itself makes you conscious and when you are conscious, you pull yourself out of the EGO'S unnecessarily over-protective attitudes.

When you are conscious, there is natural confidence. The only thing that helps us achieve results in all the spheres of our life is this consciousness that gives an inner confidence that can handle life situations powerfully, without getting impacted by anything. So the way forward is to be more and more conscious and develop confidence. Getting rid of the distractions created by the ego is also a step on the way. When disturbances are removed you are by default peaceful and confident. Confidence is built automatically when our mental and emotional blocks are removed.

Avoid reacting when similar conditions surface; let it be and keep learning on the inside. Not visiting your memories when thoughts flash is very important. Just observe the energy and not the thought. It's very important to handle emotions by having the right thoughts. Be a watchman of your thoughts. Keep creating positive thoughts.

11

Conscious Relationships

You can know that your ego is active in relationships when there is:

- Use of sharp tones.

- Non-acceptance of what is, what people say and what they do. Judging them wrongly.

- Putting people in a tight spot, correcting them all the time

- Cutting people. Making people defensive by catching their words.

- Replying literally to mere words rather than understanding the context.

- Criticising, blaming, negative thinking and fault finding.

- Use of abusive or hurtful words.

- Disturbed inner energy.

- Haphazard breathing pattern.

- Communicating everything, heightened righteousness.

- Trying to love deeply and becoming possessive.

- Inability to speak concisely, with few, sweet, slow-paced and gently spoken words.

We are the World

People are all the same at the core. Anything spoken out of unawareness triggers the unawareness in others. Psychologically everybody is the same, only actions seem to differ.

We have the same brains but we don't see it the same way because we have been competing with each other, artificially marking the brains as different. It is so evident that across the world human beings are suffering. We are living in a world of shortage; there is so much anxiety, fear, insecurity, confusion, mental illnesses, fear of getting hurt (emotionally and physically) and fear of death.

Initially, I tried to stay away from what I didn't like in people and realised that I felt very uncomfortable. I resisted a lot to accept what I didn't like in others. The transformation came when I started seeing myself in my friends, my parents, my neighbours, and the world as an extension of myself, like my hands. The engine, the brain, is the same in all of us with just a difference in our interpretations, which is the root cause of all fights and conflicts around us. Once you start seeing yourself in others, you will not have to change anybody.

Other people have their conditionings, we have ours.

They react to our conditionings; we see their reaction and not the reason behind it, which could be us or the way they see us.

We want to feel included in our circles all the time, accepted by people and for this we try to be significant and instead get excluded from our groups. Psychologically, our attempts to gain significance put us on a higher pedestal and others around us on a lower one. This gives a boost to our ego. The ego feels great in defeating people. Whereas when you drop the significance, you reach the other person's level and are included by default. Significance is trying to be important or standing out from the rest. People are selling their happy stories all the time, they have become salesmen. Our naturalness is almost lost as people are more interested in showing us how happy they are by posting pictures on Facebook than in actually being happy. This has made us dependent on how many "likes" we receive for a social media post.

When the race to earn money and respect is over, we genuinely pursue what we, in our consciousness, want to do. When you think of making others win, contributing to the larger game, and accept their weaknesses, you surpass the ego and reach the natural state of consciousness.

You feel uncomfortable even amongst your own people because the ego has many expectations and gets hurt easily. With your own people the baggage that you carry is almost constant and much more than it is with strangers. But when you become aware and there is attention in the present, egoistic thoughts cease to make an impact. When you are able to practice this for some time, you will stop deriving pleasure from other people's losses. Once your expectations drop, you naturally feel happy with people and the relationship then can be enjoyed at a much different level.

World Reflects What We Are

Once a dog ran into a museum where all the walls, the ceiling, the door and even the floor were made of mirrors. Seeing this, the dog froze in surprise in the middle of the hall, a whole pack of dogs surrounding it on all sides, from above and below. The dog bared his teeth and all the reflections responded to it in the same way. Frightened, the dog frantically barked. The reflections imitated the bark and resounded many times. The dog barked even harder and the echo kept on building. The dog tossed from one side to another, biting the air – his reflections also tossed around snapping their teeth. Next day in the morning, the museum security guards found the miserable dog, lifeless and surrounded by an equally lifeless million reflections. There was nobody who would have harmed the dog. The dog died fighting his own reflections. There is no one who is good or evil. Everything that is happening around us is the reflection of our own thoughts, feelings, wishes and karmas. The negativity that stands between you and the right path is solely yours and not theirs.

Right Action

When you have attention, you have energy and the thoughts lose control. So disruptive thoughts don't operate anymore and the birth of right action takes place. Anything you do with an agenda or a planned outcome leads to pain as agendas and outcomes lie in the future and bliss in the present. All outcome-oriented actions are actually reactions to thoughts of tomorrow. The present is the place and when you act from it, it is appropriate and not in duality. Otherwise the mind keeps thinking "was what I did right or not" as the mind struggles with the past and the future. Mind is a duality. It operates for the future wanting or not wanting what it experienced in the past. It either wants to repeat the good past or run away from the bad one. However, both keep you in the past.

Right action is not possible when you are suffering because of uncertainty, unhappiness, insecurity, greed, envy, competitiveness and violence. Right actions are possible when the suffering stops coming from your own thoughts and feelings.

What is An Illusion?

Illusion is nothing else but the opinion of the present situation and therefore one is unable to see the fact as it is. For example, if your son does not listen to you and wants to pursue a course which you don't approve of, then instead of understanding what the son wants to do, you start going on and on about the disadvantages of doing that course. You voice out your opinions instead of seeing why the son wants to do that course. This is illusion, the reality is that your son wants to do a course and you should first see and listen to his point of view rather than forcing yours.

Fact, on the other hand, is something which is actually happening. For example, "I am suffering from high fever" is a fact and "I will be cured when I fast and abstain from eating for nine days" is an illusion or "Lord Krishna will save me" is an illusion. That you are unhappy, greedy, or angry might all be actual facts but when you say, "Someone will save me from this" is an illusion.

Thoughts don't always create illusions, but all illusions are created by thoughts.

How to Be a Good Observer

When in public, observe your need to prove something, when with friends see the comparisons you make, when with parents see how you try to fix situations so that it doesn't reflect badly on you, when scared see how the ego justifies your acts, see how you wonder whether or not people are looking at you, always seeking attention, see your thoughts about others, about yourself, about life. See how the ego keeps judging you internally, your actions, decisions and behaviour. People kill animals and then pray, "Thank you for feeding us." It's their ego that protects them from going into guilt mode. The ego always wants to be morally upright instead of correcting its own actions. It does not correct them because it is made through attachments. So it cannot correct itself by default. It is attached to what it feels is right for it, irrespective of the results it is getting.

You need a sharp mind to observe things but it is blunt because it is always running and we have not given it any rest. Once you will have the sharpness of the mind, you will be able to observe the movements of your thoughts.

Observe every bit of you. Just watch the way you walk, talk, smile, laugh, cry, behave, the words you use, the decisions you make, the food you eat, alcohol you consume, the cigarettes you smoke, your relationship, your image in your own eyes, the way people see you, your attempts at defining yourself through success and the clothes you wear. Just be present totally to yourself, your intentions, your conditionings, thoughts, the way you think, the things you like, dislike, your preferences, your judgments about others, about yourself, the way you perceive things, the way you assume things, your beliefs, your habits and everything that is you and related to you. The moment you become present towards all this, without getting caught in opinions and judgments, a transformation will take place. Of course the intensity with which you observe will determine the speed at which the transformation will happen.

**What is true for you is what you have observed yourself.
And when you lose that, you have lost everything.**

12

This is it!

The ego keeps modifying things to its liking and takes control. The ego is the troublemaker as it keeps saying, "Do this and don't do that". It only desires security and respect. Our life is in disorder because the ego continuously dictates the exact opposite of what you do or what happens to you in your head as it is expecting the past experiences to repeat all the time. The only way out of the ego's misery is to understand that this uncontrollable life of ours is created by the ego itself. The ego's job is to only search for security and this quest is making us insecure.

If our minds work efficiently and rationally we feel happy but we are not aware of this. We are present to pleasures and entertainment that come from outside. Instead of working on the ego because of which we experience insecurity, we work on people, situations and collecting material things in the hope of finding happiness.

The moment you accept that life is completely uncertain, you become psychologically secure. If you try to accept the uncertainty like a concept, it won't help. But if you experience it like a fact then your mind and the ego will stop seeking greener pastures.

"In" is the Only Way "Out"

If you look closely, security is not to be found in things but within us. If I get the experience from something then I will become dependent on it. And this very dependence is what creates insecurity. Our lives are examples of the same. We are totally dependent on money, relationships and things for security.

The moment we realise that there is absolute chaos in our lives as we are depending on external things for pleasure, we can reject depending on them and experience safety and order. Security means being perceptive of the cause of insecurity, which is occupying the mind and acting from the past knowledge.

Once you understand this charade, it is over and you feel great vitality and energy. We have been wasting our energy on these insecurities and therefore don't have the energy required to handle present situations and life issues. We have to move away from the ego centre from where we are currently thinking, feeling and acting. This centre will always be in conflict with the present. In this ego's centre there will always be the need for control, which will create aggression and repression.

The whole idea of being aware and becoming conscious about the consciousness is to leave this centre of the ego that is interfering with the present. If you are able to see the whole movement of thoughts coming from experience and knowledge becoming the ego, you are out of it.